At The Boundaries

At The Boundaries

Proceedings of the Northeastern University Center for Literary Studies

Vol. 1, 1983

*Herbert L. Sussman,
Editor*

Department of English, Northeastern University
360 Huntington Avenue, Boston, Massachusetts 02115

Distributed by Northeastern University Press

© Copyright 1984, Department of English
Northeastern University

PN85.A8 1983
801'.95
LC83-21007

Table of Contents

Preface   vii

Literary Criticism as Social Diagnosis   1
Gerald Graff

Response   16
Richard Ohmann

At the Boundaries: Barthes and Derrida   23
Jonathan Culler

Response   41
Morton W. Bloomfield

What Is a Literary Text?   47
Joseph Margolis

Response   73
Susan Rubin Suleiman

Preface

In 1982–1983 the Center for Literary Studies sponsored a group of three symposia on the topic, "The Boundaries of Literary Criticism." Professors Gerald Graff, Professor and Chairman of the Department of English, Northwestern University; Jonathan Culler, Professor of English and Comparative Literature, Cornell University; and Joseph Margolis, Professor of Philosophy, Temple University, were the Center's speakers. Respondents were, in the same order, Professors Richard Ohmann, Professor of English, Wesleyan University; Morton W. Bloomfield, Professor of English, Harvard University; Susan Rubin Suleiman, Associate Professor of French, Harvard University. This volume collects the papers presented at the meetings.

While the unity of the volume did not occur by premeditated design, all three of the principal essays, in the words of a reviewer, "have in common a fascination with the work of Derrida," although other contemporary critics such as Fish, Gadamer, and Iser come under scrutiny as well. The essays in this volume make it amply clear that there is an intense concern among scholars with the issues of boundaries as delineators of the artistic work and the critical responses to it.

The Center for Literary Studies Committee wishes to thank President Kenneth Ryder, Dean Richard Astro, and those other members of the faculty and staff through whose support and efforts the work of the Center has been accomplished.

Center for Literary Studies Committee

Herbert L. Sussman, Chairperson
Irene R. Fairley
Stuart Peterfreund
Jane Nelson
Kinley E. Roby

Gerald Graff
Literary Criticism as Social Diagnosis

The recent turn toward theory in the humanities has inevitably revived questions of politics. For if "theory" means a higher degree of self-reflection about the assumptions and practices of the disciplines, it necessarily entails the reinspection of foundations; and the reinspection of foundations, in its turn, leads to the insistence on the socially-produced character of these foundations. In literary criticism, texts, authorial intentions, interpretations, and the concepts and instruments of theory are no longer viewed as givens but come to be seen as historical and social products, and sometimes as servants of institutions and interests. Certainly one prominent theme marking the recent efflorescence of literary theory is that ideas, methods, and entities heretofore felt to be "natural" resources of criticism and scholarship are in fact products of history and forms of social practice. The very categories through which readers naively make sense of texts are said to owe their authority less to any justification in the nature of texts than to conventions and practices determined by power and desire. It becomes a commonplace of the more advanced forms of criticism that no textual theory or practice is "innocent," that all theory and practice have social motives and effects. And the commonsensical scholarly assurance of the previous generation in the reliable existence of intentions, texts, and more or less credible interpretations is indicted for complacently ignoring the fact that these seemingly fixed entities have been brought into being by power and violence, and that power and violence might therefore unmake them.

Such considerations have set the tone of recent discussions of the politics of criticism and interpretation. Another kind of politics has long figured in literary criticism, however, which has yet to receive equal attention. In becoming sensitized to hidden, repressed, and oblique kinds of politics in criticism we may be in danger of overlooking a kind of politics that has operated right under our noses. Shrewd enough, even perhaps overshrewd, in rooting out the politics that resides in the motivations and consequences of literary criticism, we tend to ignore the politics which resides in its explicit *arguments*. We need only examine the kinds of justifications provided for theories of literature and criticism to see how frequently such theories depend on premises about society, premises often taken for granted rather than defended. In the modern period, i.e., since the later eighteenth century, characterizations of modern society—under such names as "bourgeois society," "commerce," "industrialism," "technology," "rationalization," etc.—have loomed large in the background of thinking about literature (as well as of literature itself). More precisely, these characterizations do not always remain in the background—they sometimes play a formative role in the way literature is conceived, or the way specific works are interpreted.

For some time, theories about the nature of literature—about the relation it has, or fails to have, to extraliterary reality, or about its mode of meaning—have been recommended on the grounds that their social consequences are more beneficial than those of competing theories. Thus the theory that literary works have a mimetic relation to the real world is praised by some because it credits literature with humanistic cultural effects, while it is damned by others for making literature an instrument of philistinism. The choice between theories which grant literature an important mimetic function and those which seek to deny or minimize that function has seemed sometimes to rest less on any empirical examination of literary works than on a choice between competing social ideals. In other cases, a diagnosis of society becomes the primary rationale for conclusions about literature, as when the view that modern society suffers from a poverty of moral ideas stimulates the thesis that literature is essentially moral or mimetic, or when the view that modern society is being stifled by morality gives rise to the thesis that literature properly transcends moral concerns.

Conspicuous examples of such arguments-from-sociology can be found amid the series of heated debates which have erupted recently over the determinacy or indeterminacy of literary texts. One needn't read deeply in the critics who have been questioning the norms of determinacy, objectivity, and validity in interpretation to sense that their attacks frequently arise from a political animus, hidden or overt. The very terminology in which the debates are conducted, in which words such as "privilege," "authority," "control," "autonomy," and "freedom" are used by all parties, indicates that social as well as literary matters are felt to be at stake, even in the most rarefied theoretical discussions. Some of the more radical critics don't hesitate to make political charges against believers in objective interpretation, arguing that insofar as interpretation is considered to be susceptible even to merely relative standards of objectivity, the cause of authoritarianism is advanced. When such a thing as a "correct" or even "more correct" interpretation is believed to exist, it is said, professors are then empowered to suppress unorthodox interpreters, whether those be their students or competing professional groups. Furthermore, insofar as objectivity is held to be a possible or desirable goal, those outside the university in control of the public machinery of interpretation can then impose their privileged interpretations of events on dissenters.

On the other side of the polemical divide, humanist critics also resort to sociological arguments, stating that, far from encouraging blind authoritarianism, objective norms are needed in order to prevent it. For if such norms are liquidated, these humanists argue, then Might would make Right—there would be no rational ground for challenging an accepted interpretation or theory. Thus both determinists and indeterminists in the current dispute have made a primary issue of the social consequences which they allege would follow from one theory or the other, with the implication that what theory of determinacy or interpretation we choose hinges on what social consequences follow from it. But this seems an anomalous conclusion; at least we would not normally suppose that the merits of a theory of literature or of interpretation could depend on the social consequences which follow from it. Whether literary works can be interpreted or not in line with some kind of objective standard seems to be a different question from that of what particular consequences follow, for pedagogy or society in general, if they can or can't be so interpreted. In a similar fashion, whether literary works make reference to extraliterary reality or not appears to be a different question from that of whether certain philistine elements of bourgeois society are encouraged or discouraged if they do or don't. In other words, insofar as theorists have their eye on the social consequences of theories in deciding which theories to prefer, they are in danger of confusing theoretical with practical issues. This is not to say that theory doesn't have an important practical dimension; obviously it does, insofar as theories always arise within a specific practical situation and always have practical consequences. But to make the practical consequences of a theory—as derived from some set of conjectures about the state of society—a primary reason for choosing it over other theories is to risk a kind of horse-before-the-cart confusion. The truth of a theory becomes secondary to its hypothetical social value, or truth simply becomes a function of social value.

At the very least, this confusion of truth and social value tends to paralyze critical debate. For if critics think they are disagreeing over the nature of literature or interpretation when in fact they are disagreeing, at least in part, over what type of society literature or interpretation ought to be encouraging, disagreements are unlikely to operate on the same level and critics will seem to be talking *past* one another rather than *to* one another. If the real issue in current debates over interpretation is not what the nature of texts are, or whether meanings are fixed or unfixed, but what the goals of the literature curriculum ought to be or what kind of society we ought to be trying to bring into being, such very different issues will have to be separated before the participants can begin to see what it is that divides them, much less go on to

5
Criticism as Social Diagnosis

pursue their disagreements fruitfully. Since it's possible to argue that both determinists and indeterminists have a certain measure of truth on their competing sides, that is, that there is a certain valid sense in which textual meanings are fixed and a certain valid sense in which they are open and variable, one may feel with some justification that the recent theoretical imbroglio over determinacy is somewhat beside the point, that what really divides the parties to the quarrel is a disagreement over the proper goals of the humanistic disciplines. That this essentially social and pedagogical quarrel has been displaced into a quarrel about literary theory may have impeded us from getting very far in it.

Certainly one lately senses a great circularity and futility descending over many of these recent arguments, in which each side so easily reduces the enemy's position to a species of political bad faith. On the one hand, those who believe that literature or interpretation can be held accountable to some reality—whether phenomenal or textual—independent of themselves can be denounced for their bourgeois need for security and reassurance. On the other hand, turning this accusation on its head, the targets of such criticism can charge those who want to do away with all such norms of accountability with a fashionable guilt over the exercise of authority. To every post-structuralist denunciation of the cowardly humanist's need for a security blanket of determinate meanings or mimetic truths, the humanist can reply by accusing the post-structuralist of a familiar kind of liberal self-hatred. Either side can be plausibly characterized as "reactionary" from the point of view of the other side, at which point theoretical controversy becomes a species of psychopolitical mud-wrestling in which any position can make cowards of us all.

I do not want to imply, however, that there is something especially new or current about the projection of political arguments into literary theory. Plato had political grounds for wanting to refute poets' claims that they represented reality, though Plato had independent philosophical arguments for asserting that these claims were false. That is, Plato didn't confuse the question of poetry's truth with the question of poetry's social effects, though his views on the one were clearly related to his views on the other, and though one can, if one wishes, argue that Plato's disparaging view of the truth-claims of poetry are an "ideologically" motivated attempt to rid the polis of potential forces of disruption. Modern theorizing about literature, however, operates in a climate very different from that of Plato or—to propound a generalization I can't pause here to defend—of any pre-romantic thinker. For in modern theory, the sense of social crisis is so much more pronounced that it becomes far more difficult than previously to keep sociological considerations from explicitly conditioning theoretical ideas. For one thing, modern theorizing is practiced under the shadow of a social order perceived by most theorists as systematically alien, indifferent, or hostile to literature itself, a society given over to practical, utilitarian, and commercial preoccupations. The consciousness of an alien environment is not merely an extrinsic condition of modern theorizing, however, for this consciousness becomes a principal determinant of theoretical argument itself. To pursue the point fully, one would have to look closely at the development of the modern "literary culture" into what has been called an "adversary culture," that is, an institution systematically committed to opposing the modes of thought, styles, epistemologies, ethics, and general intellectual paradigms felt to characterize "conventional" or "established" society. Once literature and criticism became part of an adversary culture, the very project of defining literature, along with other theoretical and practical activities of critics, was caught up in the larger problem of determining literature's social function, which is to say, its adversarial or corrective role. To be sure, the question of literature's social function had always been of concern to critics, but in the modern period, both the question itself and the degree of urgency with which it was posed took on a new character. For the idea of "society" itself had taken on new meaning in a culture beginning to understand the lessons of modern historical thinking; and the urgency of the crisis of society made it especially difficult for critics to keep this crisis separate from other issues. In short, the modern critic, in a way not true of his predecessors, was perforce a kind of amateur or closet social diagnostician. He could hardly speak or write about literature without becoming embroiled in diagnoses of various kinds of the crisis of modern society. The prophetic strain which runs so conspicuously through romantic poetics, sometimes eventuating in a near-equation of poetry with religion, could hardly have existed without grounding itself in characterizations and analyses of the supposedly fallen society to which aesthetic prophecy was supposed to minister. These conditions were responsible for endowing on criticism itself a certain heroism, and they help explain the intense excitement and attractiveness that since the romantic period has attached itself to the critical role. But they also account for certain confusions. The business of trying to determine what literature is, and how it should be understood and interpreted, became so tied to the business of determining what was wrong with society that it was easy to overlook the fact that the two projects—literary theory and social diagnosis—were not necessarily identical.

We can make the above generalizations a bit more specific by looking at some of Shelley's reasoning in the *Defence of Poetry*. For Shelley is one of those critics who, in a way that would be much copied by later ones, tied his idea of the nature of poetry to a certain analysis of the trouble with modern industrial society. Shelley's equation of the poetic spirit with such qualities as love, sympathy, and the "going out of our own nature and an identification of ourselves with the beautiful which exists in thought, action, or person not our own," would seem inexplicable or arbitrary if we did not know that Shelley was reacting against the industrial commercialism of his time. Indeed, he explicitly makes poetry, defined as the epitome of selflessness and renunciation, into the antidote for what he calls "the selfish and calculating principle." "Poetry and the principle of self of which money is the visible incarnation," he writes, "are the God and Mammon of the world."

Of course the fact that Shelley should resort to mythical references such as "Mammon" might lead one to object that it is not his own historical situation which Shelley has in mind in the *Defence* but rather an eternal and transhistorical moral opposition between the forces of good and evil. Yet Shelley could hardly have failed to recognize that "Mammon" was taking on a new and unprecedented form in his particular period, and that the forces of good, embodied in such characteristics as selflessness and sympathetic imagination, had come up against a new kind of enemy.

Thus it seems fair to say that his way of conceiving poetry is sharply present-oriented, that he derives the characteristics of poetry through a kind of negative dialectic in which the advancing evils of industrial capitalism are isolated and turned inside-out. The nature of "poetry" is given in the characteristics of "Mammon" inverted, so that poetry becomes the repository of whatever industrial society is not, or of whatever qualities of thought, feeling, and perception for which industrial society is felt by Shelley and other intellectuals to have no use.

Nor is this merely a hypothetical or theoretical matter. Major changes in poetic practice and taste are entailed by it. Shelley's reaction against the acquisitive spirit of capitalism explains his disapproval of didactic forms, forms which had not seemed so objectionable to neo-classical poets and critics and to their precursors. The didactic poet for Shelley is the poet who advances "his own conceptions of right and wrong," which is to say, the didactic method is selfish or Mammon-oriented. Shelley can thus praise *Paradise Lost* on what might otherwise seem the inexplicable ground that Milton's poem is marked by "a bold neglect of direct moral purpose." What Shelley has in mind, of course, is an imputed identification of Milton with the alien figure of Satan, an identification which Shelley sees as transcending Milton's doctrinally orthodox purpose of justifying the ways of God to man. The motivation for this "misprison" of Milton's work, the principle that imaginative sympathy with the alien and other is more deeply "moral" than any merely correct doctrinal morality, would soon become the inner rationale for a series of formal revolutions in poetry that have not ceased yet.

Of course what Shelley thought of as an attempt to get *out of* the confinements of the self eventually came to seem, to writers of T.S. Eliot's generation, all too patently a form of self-absorption. Different epochs have different ideas of what counts as self-renunciation, which is to say they have different conventions for embodying self-renunciation. When Eliot attacked Shelley and the romantic poets in general for indulging their personalities, he neglected to note that the poetics of impersonality he was invoking was only an extension of the poetics which Shelley and other romantics had originated. And what is more to my point, Eliot's version of the poetics of escape-from-egotism was conditioned no less than Shelley's by a diagnosis of society as sunk into commercial individualism. Eliot's view that meaning in poetry ought to emerge out of dislocation and disjunction derived from a diagnosis which saw dissociation and anarchy as the characteristic atmosphere of modern society.

But the comparison of Shelley's and Eliot's poetics will help me make my point about the risks accruing from the conflation of sociology and poetics. Unlike Shelley, Eliot fully acknowledged that the innovations in poetic technique that he was pioneering, as well as the theories with which he justified them, were adaptations to a particular, local "situation at hand," as he termed it, a particular socio-historical circumstance. He did not claim, at least not most of the time, that his observations on the impersonality of poetry, or on the need of the poet to "dislocate language into meaning", were defining characteristics of poetry *as such*, in all times and places. In fact, far from proposing his statements about poetry as "theories" of the nature of poetry in general, Eliot expressed embarrassment when his *ad hoc* principles were later elevated by the New Criticism into categorical definitions. Shelley by contrast, is not so aware as Eliot that the qualities he ascribes to poetry are essentially *recommendations* addressed to a local, historical situation, and he puts forth his recommendations as definitive statements about poetry in all times and places.

The procedure is not wholly misguided. Had Shelley not looked at the history of poetry with spectacles colored by his peculiar historical experience, he would not have been alert to an aspect of *Paradise Lost* which others (with the exception of Blake, who anticipated Shelley's "Satanist" interpretation of the poem) had ignored. One might say that it was only because Shelley had a certain social ax to grind that he was able to read *Paradise Lost* in a new way, or perhaps perceive something in the old way of reading it that had not been noticed. At least insofar as one believes that Milton does express a certain sympathy for the "Devil's party," whether that be through his subconscious or by virtue merely of Satan's spectacular presence in the work, one can argue that Shelley's historically-biased perspective enabled him to make an important discovery about the poem.

On the other hand, if Shelley is right about *Paradise Lost* he's right for the wrong reasons, and in a way that threatens to do anachronistic violence to the work. For by comparison with Shelley, Milton had no particlar ax to grind against "Mammon." Nor did Milton, either in his treatment of Satan or in any other part of the poem, think that he was writing "poetry" in Shelley's sense, where poetry is a counterprinciple to the forces of competitive egotism. If Milton did think in something like these terms they would for him be colored by Christian notions of Original Sin and thus significantly different in social and moral temper from Shelley's. Milton had no need to conceive egotism or Mammon in the same terms as Shelley, and thus no need to conceive poetry in the same terms. Shelley's general remarks about poetry may help illuminate parts of Milton's poem but in the main they are irrelevant to it. Nor is this surprising, for there is no reason to think that ideas derived from the exigencies of a particular historical situation should apply to poetry as such.

If Shelley's example is as typical as I think it is of the direction of modern literary theory, then a good deal of that theory should be understood not as "theory" at all, in the sense of a descriptive analysis of the nature of literature, but rather as a set of prescriptions or recommendations regarding what literature (or criticism) *ought* to be in the light of a certain diagnosis of society. And indeed, one could go further and argue that the proliferation of a multiplicity of different "theories" of literature in the modern period is in part a reflection of the multiplicity of different social diagnoses, each of which dialectically generates its own counter-conception of literature. For modern society being what it is, the number of deficiencies which can be plausibly adduced as its central deficiencies is very large. And since modern society is contradictory, diagnoses—and hence theories of poetry—will eventually contradict one another.

It's possible to sketch a typology of these conflicting theories of literature by distinguishing the disparate forms of cultural complaint which have generated them. Thus there is the large number of theories from Kant and Shelley down through various New Critics and formalists which have conceived literature (or art in general) in terms of *disinterestedness.* Invariably such theories see literature as a counterweight against a social order felt to be overrun by competitive aggression and acquisitiveness. Over against these theories, however, we would have to set those for which literature, far from being viewed as a disinterested mode, is seen as a kind of cure for the overidealized sickliness of disinterestedness. Whereas the one group of critics defines literature as an *antidote for* the will-to-power which rules society, the other defines it as the *expression of* that will-to-power, against a society which tries hypocritically to deny its primacy. Both groups conceive literature as the dialectical "other" of bourgeois society, but since their diagnoses of "bourgeois society" are different, their conceptions of literature differ.

Shifting the axis slightly in order to illustrate the same point, we could list the innumerable critics who have viewed modern society as a vast *disorder* and who consequently see literature as the compensatory orderer, the means by which lost unity and oneness are recovered. On the other side we would then have to list the equally numerous critics who have found modern society as *all too orderly*, as in fact rigorously regimented, programmed, and dominated by stock perceptions and stereotyped categories. It is from these critics that we tend to get theories of literature as utopian disruption, perceptual defamiliarization, high-energy discharge, erotic release, cognitive dissonance, and (most recently) deconstructive dissemination and self-undoing. Again, literary theories generated by such diagnoses (which are often more taken for granted than expounded) are not theories at all in the descriptive or analytic sense so much as strategic recommendations made on the basis of a reaction against a particular aspect of society. There are always arguments to be made both for and against such recommendations, for modern society is probably *both* too orderly and too disorderly in about equal measure, though the terms can be manipulated so as to make one characteristic predominate.

That critics of thirty years ago tended to favor the diagnosis of excessive disorder may help explain why they "valorized" the organic unity of literary works as an allegedly defining characteristic. That most up-to-date recent critics favor the diagnosis of excessive order may explain why they valorize disunity as a special quality of literature, or perhaps of all utterances. Both approaches have an *a priori* character, the one positing in advance that great literary works will be unified, the other, that they will not be; both approaches yield interesting and true observations about some literary works while ignoring or falsifying works which don't fit their descriptions. But again, such approaches are not descriptions at all so much as prescriptions aimed at rectifying through literature and criticism what is viewed as a cultural deficiency. Of course the fact that works of literature themselves are written according to such prescriptions further complicates the matter: the creation of New Critical or deconstructionist poems or novels appears to vindicate New Critical or deconstructionist theories. But no amount of new creation can obliterate the history of literature, which is to say the immense variety of very different things which have gone under the name of "literature" and which can't be subsumed under monolithic ideas of unity or disunity.

I've been arguing that much of the sociology introduced by literary critics into their work is logically irrelevant to what they believe themselves to be doing, i.e., theorizing about the nature of literature or of interpretation. But there are instances when the sociology introduced by literary critics is not logically irrelevant so much as *empirically dubious*. (It can, of course, be both.) Take, for example, Derrida's statement that there is one thing which the "pedagogical institution cannot bear," and this is

> for anyone to tamper with language, meaning both the national language and, paradoxically, an ideal of translatability that neutralizes this national language. Nationalism and universalism. What this institution cannot bear is a transformation that leaves intact neither of these two complementary poles. It can bear more readily the most apparently revolutionary ideological sorts of "content," if only that content does not touch the borders of language and of all the juridico-political contracts that it guarantees. It is this "intolerable" something that concerns me here.[1]

Derrida understands that he is making a practical argument for transgressing the conventional "borders of language"—quite apart from the theoretical arguments he so copiously develops elsewhere in his work. His case against linguistic boundaries here is not that the metaphysics of presence on which they rest is questionable philosophically, but that this metaphysics of presence legitimates the "juridico-political contracts" through which the university and the larger society wield power and authority. By Derrida's account, transgression of the borders of language constitutes transgression of the linguistic and conceptual assumptions which keep established institutions intact. Thus he assumes that deconstructive "tampering" with language must be systematically resisted.

Clearly the merits of Derrida's tactical defense of deconstruction, if not of his thought as a whole, rest on the persuasiveness of this last assumption that the university and other institutions are of such a nature that they can't tolerate linguistic de-centering. For only if this is the case could anybody suppose that deconstructive "de-centering" could be tactically effective. Is this assumption credible, however? Is it true that the university "cannot bear" deconstructive tampering with language? Has it not tolerated a certain measure of tampering so far? As for the university's supposed commitment to universality, it's a common observation that the university has become so fragmented in its proliferation of autonomous specialized vocabularies that no common metalanguage has been able to give coherence to the whole. If the university actually encouraged translatability across disciplinary vocabularies, one imagines advocates of interdisciplinary integration would encounter fewer obstacles to their reforms than they do. Derrida correctly perceives something "paradoxical" in the combination of "nationalism and universalism" which once existed in the university. What he doesn't consider is that both nationalism and universalism may have been seriously eroded by the heterogeneity of specialized professional discourses. One might argue that far from being organized around a centralized or universalist model, the modern university is something of a deconstructionist. It proliferates textual vocabularies which can't be tamed to the common measure of any metalanguage. If the university nevertheless exerts a conservative political force, as it arguably does, might this be not by repressively policing the "juridico-political contracts" of language, as Derrida suggests, but rather by dissolving these linguistic contracts in a way which keeps everyone too confused to act or even to formulate issues clearly?

Of course Derrida's remarks are addressed to the situation in French universities—it is Derrida's American followers who carry them over and apply them to the universities in the United States. One danger of borrowing our critical ideas from France is that the situation which inspired these ideas may hardly exist in our country, where the university has never been tied to the centralized power of church and state, and where traditional high culture, far from having the semi-official status it has had in France, has always regarded itself as a rather despised outsider in relation to the much more powerful culture of advertising, publicity, and journalism. Professors of the humanities may affect social airs, but they feel distinctly inferior to the managers of business and the media, in comparison with whom they are poorly paid. University-based radicals have difficulty perceiving these facts, partly because their direct experience of authority is so circumscribed. If the chief form in which authority presents itself to you daily is either your dissertation director or the professor who may vote against your tenure, it may be natural enough to start feeling that those authorities are a direct continuation of other forms of authority, from the police on up to the government and the military, and that all these forms of authority share a common ideology. This is especially tempting when the professors, to hide their own sense of marginality and weakness (which is often only different in degree from that of their students), comport themselves like generalissimos and patricians. The illusions thus produced prop up the myth of the university as a haven of authoritarian centrism, which in turn fuels deconstructive radicalism.

Though Derrida's remarks may have a pertinence to the French situation that they cannot have in the United States, one wonders if they are not even then oversimplifications. For all his sophistication when he writes philosophically, when he ventures into social observation, Derrida suddenly sounds about as muddled and simple-minded as the rest of us. Could anybody deny that the passage quoted above little distinguishes itself from standard avant-garde platitudes which depict established culture as the stolid and stodgy straight-man whose pomposity and inflexibility make the avant-garde seem wonderfully outré by contrast? Surely, one imagines, the established culture could not be quite so stupidly rigid as all that and still manage to put itself over so successfully. Not that there is no possible truth in the assumption that established society is so dependent on centrist ideology that it must assign university pedants the job of holding linguistic transgressors in check. But even if true, the assumption should be tested against the competing view—less flattering to the would-be literary radical's belief in his subversive effect—that the university and corporate society long ago broke their dependency on the sorts of narrow ideologies that could seriously be threatened by deconstructive assaults on universalism and the principle of translatability. If these established agencies do operate in conservative ways, it is possible they do so not by imposing on us a single monolithic or logocentric system but rather by managing a contradictory plurality and confusion of systems. One needn't choose one model at the expense of the other—both may be simultaneously true for different moments and regions. At the very least the question should be treated as open, not foreclosed by rhetorical flourishes.

If there is any merit in my argument that the pressures of modern experience have caused literary criticism to become a form of social diagnosis, two corollaries for the practice of criticism follow. The first is that critics should try to be more alert to the distinction between the empirical or analytic aspects of their work and the political aspect, which is to say they should try to be more alert to the difference between *describing* literature and criticism, as more or less detached interpreters or theorists, and *prescribing* for literature and criticism, on the basis of an analysis of what seems most needed and beneficial for a particular social environment. Both are valid enterprises, but they are different ones and shouldn't be confused. I'm aware that some will say that this distinction between description and prescription has itself been deconstructed, is itself "ideological," repressive, and so forth. I've tried to deal with this argument elsewhere.[2] All I can say here is that I'm aware of this objection and don't think it can be stated without self-contradiction and incoherence.

As for my second corollary, it's a more obvious one: insofar as we critics base our ideas of literature on a diagnosis of social ills, it seems desirable that we know what we are talking about. The tradition of social criticism inherited by contemporary literary criticism is still essentially a nineteenth-century tradition, formed when bourgeois society was developing its classic orientations—toward utilitarianism, the subordination of the pleasure principle to the performance principle, the glorification of work over consumption, the belief in reason and the idea of progress. Insofar as this classic bourgeois society has been eroded or superseded by the very dynamisms it itself unleashed, social criticism that remains fixated on this model of society will be flogging a dead horse. It's a commonplace that we now live in a "post-modern" or "post-industrial" society which renders nineteenth-century sociological axioms obsolete or useless. Yet even though literary critics frequently restate this commonplace, some of them seem not to take it seriously enough. If the question of what our society actually is were treated as more open, literary criticism—or at least some of it— would become more tentative than it is today.

Notes

1. "Living On: Border Lines," trans. James Hulbert, *Deconstruction and Criticism*, ed. Harold Bloom (New York: Seabury Press, 1979), pp. 94–95.

2. Gerald Graff, "Textual Leftism," *Partisan Review*, 44 (1982), 558–575; also "The Pseudopolitics of Interpretation," *Critical Inquiry*, 9 (1983), 597–610.

Richard Ohmann *Response*

The genre of the public response, the thing I am doing right now, is one in which the fur is supposed to fly. As I understand this genre, a person in my position is supposed to spend maybe a minute praising the talk by saying that it is important and penetrating, and the speaker was certainly right in refuting x, y and z. And, then, as if in neon, a great big "But," followed by ten minutes of a devastating critique which leaves the paper in rubble.

17
Criticism as Social Diagnosis

I don't think I can do that today. Actually there's not very much in Graff's talk that I object to, some that I strongly endorse, like the remarks at the end about bringing conflict out where it can be explicitly and openly engaged rather than keeping it in the closet. The main point, the main theoretical point, I should say, which I'll refer to in a moment again is, in my opinion, unexceptionable and very healthy, and that is—if I can simplify it even more than he did—that one cannot derive an "is" from an "ought" by saying that literature is such and such a way because we want it to be such and such a way, any more than (the more common version of that fallacy) one can derive an "ought" from an "is," as for instance, E. D. Hirsch did in *The Philosophy of Composition*, in which he argued that we should promulgate standard languages because history had produced them for us and has continued to produce them.

So, I think that Graff is right in the theoretical point that he makes and in order to produce some flying fur or whatever, I have to move away from his main theoretical point and talk about some thoughts that it stirs, in more of a meditative than a combative response. I want to draw attention to the implications of his argument that puzzled me, and this may be worth some of our time a little bit later on when we will discuss these ideas together. I take it that Graff's contribution to theory is a point about what moves are permissible in a theoretical argument. I've just described that by saying that you can't derive an "is" from an "ought." Now, that point is made, made completely, and Graff is pretty much finished with it by about a quarter of the way through his talk, when he says that arguments of the form "If we accept theory x, cultural consequence y would follow" are simply beside the point when introduced into theoretical debates over which theories are most correct or adequate—that such arguments lead to a "horse-before-the-cart confusion."

Then he goes on, for the rest of the talk, to arguments of just this sort, against the fallacy he has exposed. For example, critical debate tends to have its focus diverted to the psychopolitical motivations of opposing theorists. That is, one bad consequence of arguing in this fallacious way is that you shift the attention over to motivations, into the psychopolitical and away from the relevant merits of theoretical arguments. Or he puts it another way, knowledge in other words is subsumed by the sociology of knowledge. That's another bad consequence of theory being done in the latest subjective terms, with the demoralizing effect that "theoretical controversy becomes a kind of psychopolitical mud-wrestling." Those seem to me to be arguments about the practical consequences of this sort of theoretical move, which he produces as an objection to that kind of theory, even though he has already to my satisfaction, proved that that's a bad kind of theoretical move *without* talking about its practical consequences.

The rest of the talk was, as I understand it, about three things that he says don't belong in this theoretical environment. One was the practical consequences—and the ones I already mentioned plus mis-communication, confused debate, proliferation of theories, including some that would contradict each other, and so on. Second, it was about the motives of the people who have argued this way, arising out of his important observation that in the last couple of hundred years or so there's been a lot of argument of this sort, and maybe that comes from the way that people talk about literature and increasingly see themselves in an antagonistic relationship with society. And third, I would say that a great deal of what he said in the last part of his talk was sociology of knowledge. I like that so I'm not objecting to it, but I thought he objected to it. So as Graff shows in the first part of his talk, none of that bears on the theoretical question of what counts as a theoretical argument.

Now, I want to go on to ask why did Graff argue in this way, immediately after showing that such arguments could not have any bearing on the theoretical point? I want to inquire about his motives. But not just his, because very many of us, including often myself, do argue that way, mixing theory with motives and practical consequences, mixing "ought" with "is." And it's sometimes in the closet and sometimes out. I'm doing it now. And I want to ask why if this is a theoretically irrelevant way to argue, we like to do it so much? And I'm going to offer the conjecture, from the non-theoretical reasons Graff cited for his theoretical argument, that his theoretical point is important to him because he has a certain social and moral ideal for literary intellectuals and for our discourse, that he cares quite a lot about it and that he sees it as being seriously undermined in recent critical debate. And recent can mean anything from the last ten years to the last couple of hundred. So that, in other words, there is an occasion for Graff's making this theoretical point, just as there often is an occasion for making theoretical points. That's O.K.

I think the ideal that can be inferred from the bad practical consequences that he says will follow from arguing this way is an ideal (maybe I'm making a caricature—I don't think so and I don't object to it either) of disinterested pursuit of truth, apart from the flow and tug of current social needs and political agendas. I think that he wants to say that there is a pure realm of discourse which can and should be defended against the intrusion of politics, at least some of the time. At least you have the purity of that discourse some of the time, so that then when you bring politics in, you can relate the two in a way that's clear and explicit.

Well, I think that's attractive but I'm wondering—this really is a wonder—whether it's a reasonable ideal of a theoretical discourse, the discourse of intellectuals. I don't dispute at all that you can separate theory from social context, even if there are social occasions always which give rise to theory. But I suspect that to the extent to which you do succeed in separating theory from social context, you tend to reduce theory to more and more abstract and purely logical discourse. And finally, all might boil down, if you carry this to an extreme, to a proposition such as x equals x, and if x entails y, and y entails z, then x entails z. In other words, you would reduce it to a kind of ghostly paradigm of argument. That is, the arguments in such a theory, which was lifted entirely of its social embeddedness, would have validity or could have validity (and we could always tell if they were valid or invalid) but would they have significance? Would we care about them? Would they have any importance to us? Would they answer to, in any way, the concerns that gave rise to the arguments in the first place? Arguments do have a logical form, but in the real world they are also speech acts, extended speech acts made in particular circumstances and with particular forces and intents and consequences. So why not, I found myself wondering, join theory and politics, so long as we would follow Graff in demanding clarity about the line that may, for some purposes and at some times, be drawn between theory and politics, when one wants to focus, for a moment, on the pure form of the argument, on its logical character and validity? That's a question I would throw out for discussion.

Finally, I want to turn your attention to a really important point Graff made at the very outset of this talk before saying that this talk isn't about it, and going on to other things. That is about the turn towards theory coinciding with the revival of interest in politics. He said that theory figures to lead inevitably to the socially produced nature of its object, of texts, interpretations, of the concepts of theory itself. I think that he welcomes that development and I do, too. What I wanted to do, though, is to try to bring that to bear on one main kind of literary theory that he kept alluding to, that is that part of literary theory that tries to say what literature is or what poetry is and to distinguish those things from other kinds of discourse. I'm one of the people who's tried his hand at that question, of what sort of discourse is literature. Partly because of my own efforts and the aftermath, but more because these questions have been rather intensively pursued for a couple of centuries, it seems to me that the results of them have been pretty discouraging. I think of what Graff said about the heterogeneity of discourses and maybe that would be a better rule of thumb to adopt than to try to find *the* defining characteristics of literary discourse which distinguish it from all the others, because the attempts to do the latter haven't succeeded very well. It makes you wonder whether the question isn't the wrong question. That question, "What is literature?" assumes, just in its structure, that literature is a well-bounded set, a set that exists partly in the future, but it is a well-bounded set, which is stable across history.

Clearly that isn't so. In the first place we didn't have any such concept as literature until fairly recently in history, and the things that have counted as literature in that recent part of our history have shifted and changed and been the focus of considerable controversy, as people like Raymond Williams and lots of others have amply shown. The theory of literature, I'm suggesting, is intrinsically either circular, in the sense that you decide what criterion you are going to use, in order to enumerate the set of things that are literature, and then you define literature in terms of the criterion you produce out of that set, the criterion that produced the set in the first place; or else it is mystifying, in that the definition of literature will deny that it is really a prescription for what kinds of literature are good literature or ought to be preferred or ought to be written, really a kind of closet canon formation in which all of the exercise of power is going on beneath the surface.

I am suggesting that maybe we could profitably, we the people who talk about this kind of thing at all, spend our time better by concentrating on the concept of literature, rather than on literature. Maybe we should study how that concept has been socially produced (because it has, over very recent history). With what human motives, and in response to what human needs, and whose needs, and to whose benefit and through what social conflict have we come to sort of know what literature is, which things belong to it, and which things are not literature, but only junk or trash or whatever else we use to contrast with literature? That would be a historical task I think, not so much a social scientific one, though obviously, I don't want to separate social science from history and from literary theory; I for one wouldn't mind seeing some of the people from Yale and Johns Hopkins and so on put aside the theoretical fancy work for a while, seeing them and the rest of us privilege instead an exploration of our ideas and texts as products of history and power. Of course such a shift in interest for us, for our profession, would bring politics out of the closet but that's O.K. with me, and I think that it is with Graff too.

Jonathan Culler | *At the Boundaries: Barthes and Derrida*

A concern with boundaries is endemic to literary criticism, and perhaps especially to literary theory. What might appear to be the primary question for literary theory, "What is literature?," invariably turns into a question about boundaries: what distinguishes the literary from the non-literary? What separates novels from histories, poems from everyday utterances? Answers to these questions attempt to settle boundaries, offering justifications for the lines they draw—between cognitive and emotive uses of language, for example, or between referential and non-referential statements. But even if one tries to ignore the question of boundaries and seeks not to delimit the class of literary works but to describe the properties of works generally deemed literary—works whose aesthetic purposes and effects are not in dispute—one finds oneself contending with a problem of boundaries once again. Theorists have been notoriously unsuccessful in discovering essential, defining properties of literary discourse; and scrupulous reflection on the nature of literature is likely to lead theorists to the conclusion that literature is not a special sort of discourse but language framed or set off in special ways.

An articulate statement of this view is presented by Barbara

Herrnstein Smith, who argues in *On the Margins of Discourse* that literary works should be seen as "fictive utterances." There are no intrinsic linguistic features that distinguish them as a class of utterances; they are to be described as fictional imitations of various sorts of non-fictional or "historical" utterances. "The various genres of literary art," Smith argues, "can to some extent be distinguished according to what types of discourse—for example, dialogues, anecdotes of past events, public speeches, and private declarations—they characteristically represent. Thus, lyric poems typically represent personal utterances."[1]

> It is as if each novel opens with the invisible words, "For example": "[For example], about thirty years ago, Miss Maria Ward of Huntington, with only seven thousand pounds, had the good luck to captivate Sir Thomas Bertram, of Mansfield Park . . .;" and as if every play opens with an invisible prologuist who says, "For example, events such as these could occur," and every lyric with the invisible words, "For example, I (or someone) could say . . ."[2]

[For example, I (or someone) could say], "That's my last duchess hanging on the wall . . ." or [For example, I (or someone) could say], "Busie old fool, unruly sunne. . . ." Literary works are distinguished by the frame of fictive exemplification.

In this account, the nature of literature is tied up with a boundary between so-called "historical" utterances and fictional imitations of them. Now if one questions Smith's notion of "historical utterance" and seeks a more explicitly aesthetic account of literature (for not all *imitations* of historical utterances would count as literary works), one's investigation of aesthetic properties still leads to frames or boundaries—to the frames which, by setting aesthetic objects off from their surroundings, constitute them as aesthetic objects, or to the boundaries that mark off purposive wholes without purpose, setting them off from purpose. In an exposition of Kant's *Critique of Judgement* entitled "Parergon," Jacques Derrida notes that aesthetic theory has been structured by a persistent demand:

> We must know what we are talking about, what concerns the value of beauty intrinsically and what remains external to an immanent sense

of beauty. This permanent demand—to distinguish between the internal or proper meaning and the circumstances of the object in question—organizes every philosophical discourse on art, the meaning of art, and meaning itself, from Plato to Heidegger. It presupposes a discourse on the boundary between the inside and the outside of the art object, in this case a discourse on the frame.[3]

The history of art, music, and literature in our own time confirms what one might infer from Derrida's investigation of Kant's aesthetic: that anything which is framed—displayed in a museum, hung in a gallery, performed on stage, printed in a book of poems—can become an art object. But if frames and framing constitute the art object, they do so not by substantive properties but by a differential marking, by the articulation of boundaries. "There is framing," remarks Derrida, "but the frame does not exist." "Il y a du cadre, mais le cadre n'existe pas" (p. 93/39). *Parergon* is one of Kant's terms for this framing element which lies outside the body of the *ergon* or work, as a supplement to it. Derrida writes:

> The *parergon* detaches itself both from the *ergon* and from the milieu; it detaches itself first as a figure against a background, but it does not set itself off in the same way as the work, which is also set off against a background. The parergonal frame detaches itself from two backgrounds, but in relation to each it backs into the other. In relation to the work, which serves as its background, it disappears into the wall and then by degrees into the general text. In relation to the background of the general text, it backs into the work which is set off from the general background. (pp. 71–73).

This description certainly applies to the picture frame which, in relation to the wall, is part of the picture, but in relation to the canvas is part of its surroundings, backs into the wall. When one moves from pictures to the framing of poems, the purely differential nature of framing becomes clear. "Always a figure against a ground," Derrida continues, "the *parergon* is nevertheless a form that has traditionally been defined not as setting itself off but as disappearing, sinking in, effacing itself, dissolving just as it expends its greatest energy. The frame is never a background as the milieu or the work can be, but neither is its thickness of margin a figure, unless a self-razing figure [*figure qui s'enlève d'elle-même*]" (pp. 72–73/25–26).

This disappearing, differential figure is nevertheless in a certain way the "essence" of art. Kant's account of beauty—in many ways strikingly odd but still paradigmatic for our sense of what is fundamentally involved in the aesthetic—proceeds by stripping away all those qualities which works of art may and quite generally do possess but which are only incidental, not essential, to their aesthetic function. The beauty that concerns judgments of pure taste is an organization that "signifies nothing, shows nothing, represents nothing." Doubtless, aesthetic structures will *also* represent, indicate, signify, but their beauty is independent of such functions, based on what Derrida calls "le *sans* de la coupure pure," the *without* of the pure break which marks aesthetic objects, as in Kant's "purposive wholes without purpose." As Derrida's pun indicates, though (*sans*: without, and *sens*: meaning or direction), the "without" of these aesthetic boundaries (in purposiveness without purpose, referentiality without reference, truthfulness without truth, and numerous other pairings that are linguistically more awkward to devise) is the meaning of this break, inducing us to talk of literature as language, or mimesis, or whatever, *cut off* from certain kinds of functioning.

The structure that gets established in our theoretical pursuit of boundaries is not one in which literature lies securely on one side of a boundary and the non-literary or the non-aesthetic on the other. On the contrary, the frame or the *sans de la coupure pure* is ubiquitous, so that literature can come to include anything that is opposed to it: identify some kind of discourse as wholly unliterary, and the chances are good that it will turn up shortly in a novel. There is nothing so definitively unliterary that it may not appear in a book of poems; so that definitions of literature have to incorporate some sort of self-transcending mechanism, whereby the boundary between the literary and the non-literary itself becomes part of literature, a topic or concern of literature. The frame that marks off literary discourse becomes itself the subject of that discourse. The questioning of the literary, the attempt to destroy literature, is a mark of literature. The novel, from the very outset, includes the parody of the novel and the theory of the novel. If literature depends upon the boundary that marks it off, separates it from the non-literary, it also repeatedly incorporates that boundary within itself, working insatiably at the boundary.

This is an account of literature that Jacques Derrida, in particular, has helped to make possible, though it is certainly implicit in a long critical tradition. But the question of the boundaries of literature is not the same as the question of the boundaries of literary criticism, to which the title of these sessions directs our attention. The latter question takes two important forms these days. First, there is much concern with boundaries or limits of interpretation: How far can critics go? Are there no limits to what critics can say these days? "There *must* be boundaries," goes the anxious claim, "or else anything goes"; and to avoid that dire condition, critical theory seeks to establish boundaries, whether by deeming certain sorts of evidence illicit or establishing principles of interpretation. But attempts to set boundaries to interpretation, like attempts to define meaningless sentences, are characteristically little more than a challenge to the self-transcending mechanisms of literary and critical consciousness to go beyond them, to bring them into the arena of critical discourse and debate. When Norman Holland, who believes that each reader recreates the work in accordance with his or her own uniquely distinctive identity theme, attempts to draw a boundary by noting that there are limits to this re-creation and that no reader, for example, could imagine that Faulkner's "A Rose for Emily" is about Eskimos, Stanley Fish replies, quite correctly, that it is very easy to imagine an "Eskimo interpretation" of the story. If, for example, we were to discover "a letter in which Faulkner confides that he has always believed himself to be an Eskimo changeling," Faulkner criticism would begin to reinterpret the Faulkner canon and elaborate a system of allusions and symbolic references that showed the texts to be informed by Eskimo meanings. "The example is absurd," Fish notes, "only if one forgets Yeats's *Vision* or Blake's Swedenborgianism or James Miller's recent elaboration of a homosexual reading of *The Waste Land*."[4]

A different example of the way attempts to set boundaries to criticism work in fact to identify a cut within criticism as a source of energy and interest is Wayne Booth's proposal that we distinguish "proper questions," which the work itself urges readers to ask, from "improper questions," that violate a text's intentions and lead not to understanding but to what he calls "overstanding."[5] "All texts," Booth argues, "try to present boundary conditions which all experienced readers will recognize. Whether all readers will choose to *honor* the boundaries is an entirely different question" (p. 242). A narrative that begins "Once upon a time there were three little pigs" demands that we ask "And *then* what happened," while such questions as "Why three?" or "Why pigs?" join Booth's list of improper questions that we "impose on" the text: for instance, "What do you have to say, you seemingly innocent child's tale of three little pigs and a wicked wolf, about the culture that preserves and responds to you? About the unconscious dreams of the author or the folk that created you? About the history of narrative suspense? About the relations of the lighter and the darker races? . . . About triadic patterns in human history?" And so on (p. 243). One can see what Booth is up to here, pluralistically conceding the interest of improper questions and "overstanding," so long as critics confess the priority of proper questions and of *under*standing; but his policing of pluralism in fact focuses our attention on the boundary of the proper and the improper, which has not been nor will be in the future a limit of criticism but is and will be a conflictual stimulus to reflection *within* criticism. I venture to suggest that almost every *proper* question, such as "What happened next?", will be critically less productive (less productive of critical discourse we find worth reading) than marginally improper questions, such as "Why three little pigs?"

Many of these "improper questions" raise the issue of the boundaries of criticism in its second form: the question of the boundary between literary criticism and other disciplines. "Once upon a time there were three little pigs" encourages forays into or out of psychology, anthropology, sociology, and so on. Such forays are controversial. Northrop Frye, in the splendid "Polemical Introduction' to the *Anatomy of Criticism*, is not concerned with keeping interpretation within what he deems reasonable bounds but with maintaining boundaries between the poetics he wishes to advance and other disciplines. "To defend the right of criticism to exist at all," he argues, "is to assume that criticism is a structure of thought and knowledge existing in its own right, with some measure of independence from the art it deals with."[6] And once we admit that the critic has his own field of activity, then "we have to concede that criticism deals with literature in terms of a specific conceptual framework." He dismisses all criticisms, "whether Marxist, Thomist, liberal-humanist, neo-classical, Freudian, Jungian, or existentialist," which propose "not to find a conceptual framework for criticism within literature but to attach criticism to one of a miscellany of frameworks outside it." The critic, he argues, must "make an inductive survey of his own field and let his critical principles shape themselves solely out of his knowledge of that field." Note how even in Frye's scientific program, the organicist language—"principles shape themselves"—bespeaks the dream of self-generation. Part of the attraction of a science of literature for Frye is that "the presence of science in any subject changes its character from casual to causal, from the random and intuitive to the systematic, as well as safeguarding the integrity of that subject from external invasions" (pp. 6–7).

Doubtless many people wish that the subject had been better safeguarded from external invasions in recent years (and might even be willing to have accepted Frye's sweet science as the price of safety from invasion, investing in Frye's modes and *mythoi* as "peacekeepers"). What Frye calls external invasion is my subject this afternoon, although I think that to speak of external invasion is to misunderstand the situations of both literature and criticism, which exist at the boundaries, in disputes about boundaries.

Let us note, first, that despite Frye's call for a criticism whose principles shape themselves from within, even Frye's own criticism was not able to develop in this way, and much of its *effect* seems to have been tied to its use of transliterary mythological categories. Frye's example in fact inspired critics not to work out a pure poetics but to develop Myth criticism, which described literary works in terms of archetypes seen as fundamental to human experience of the world. If these trans- or supraliterary categories are responsible for his criticism's greatest success, there may be a lesson there about external invasions and the importance of defending boundaries at all costs.

Certainly the recent history of criticism suggests that energy and insight come from the interaction between the literary and the non-literary. Linguistics, philosophy, psychoanalysis, feminism, and Marxism are the discourses that have done most to stimulate literary criticism; but Frye's fears that criticism might come to be lodged *within* some disciplinary framework have not been realized. Nor, I think, is it really the case that criticism has become dependent upon the methods and concepts of linguistics, philosophy, or psychoanalysis, for example. The relation is a more complicated one in which borrowed terms and categories enable one to see literary phenomena in a new light but are themselves affected by the kind of analyses in which they become engaged, and can in turn provide a new perspective on the phenomena of the discipline from which they were originally drawn. As theorists know only too well, linguists, philosophers, and psychoanalysts are swift to disown and condemn the "literary applications" of their concepts and methods; though literary theorists, for their part, maintain that the inflection given to concepts borrowed by literary studies often makes possible a more insightful exploration of linguistic, philosophical, or psychoanalytic matters than one gets from the "proper" and disciplinarily orthodox use of these concepts. Derrida's work enables one to argue, for example, that the most philosophically effective readings of philosophical texts are literary ones: readings that treat philosophical concepts as textual strategies and tropes. Derrida's analyses suggest that so-called philosophical texts are most acute and precise when their figures and rhetorical strategies are given close attention, and, conversely, that texts usually identified as "literary" reveal powerful philosophical deconstructions once the functioning of their special logics, such as the logic of *supplementarity*, is revealed.

The case of Roland Barthes, my other worker at the boundaries, suggests not only the fruitfulness of applying all sorts of concepts and disciplines to literature—more than any other contemporary critic, Barthes exploits the *Verfremdungseffekt* of terms from other disciplines—but also the way a literary perspective can challenge and modify concepts borrowed from elsewhere, to make them more adequate to their object. For example, Barthes was an early advocate of semiology. In *Mythologies* he discovered that various linguistic terms could give him a new perspective on cultural phenomena, and he enthusiastically embraced the possibility of studying all human activity as a series of "languages." Part of the attraction of a semiology was the hope that a formal discipline which required one to name signifiers and signifieds would display convincingly the ideological contents of various activities. But the point of a new discipline or new vocabulary was above all to force one to look closely at what goes without saying: in order to apply the new terms or perform the new operations one must rethink familiar practices. Linguistics played this role for Barthes, but by the time he became Professor at the Collège de France, Barthes's semiotic investigations had led him to see semiotics not as the application of linguistic concepts to other domains but as a critique or undoing of linguistics: more specifically, as the study of all aspects of signification set aside as impure by a scientific linguistics. Semiology, he writes, is "the labor that collects the impurity of language, the waste of linguistics, the immediate corruption of any message: nothing less than the desires, fears, expressions, intimidations, advances, blandishments, protests, excuses, aggressions, and melodies of which active language is made."[7] The application of a linguistic model to the study of literature and other cultural phenomena does not lead, as Frye seemed to fear, to a take-over of literary criticism by linguistics, but rather to a literarily-inspired critique of linguistics for its inadequacy to certain aspects of language.

Barthes as literary critic is always a worker at the boundaries. In *Leçon*, his inaugural lecture at the Collège de France, he jokes that he hopes to make his Chair of Literary Semiology into a wheelchair, always on the move, "the wildcard [joker] of contemporary knowledge" (p. 38). His choice of authors is idiosyncratic. His first book, *Le Degré zéro de l'écriture* celebrates self-conscious, modernist literary projects, and one imagines its author turning next to Camus or to Blanchot—contemporaries attempting to practice the anti-literature he had described. Instead he takes up Jules Michelet, a prolific, popular historian of the early nineteenth century, a colorful writer and ardent patriot, admirer of the French Revolution and of a picturesque, mysterious Middle Ages, which he chronicled in numerous volumes of imaginative history. Michelet's writing lacks the self-conscious literary experimentation Barthes claims to admire, and for Barthes to make him the object of his first sustained work of criticism is a perverse testing of the textual canon. Though Barthes later writes about Racine and Balzac, the other authors who get most space are three whom few had ever thought literary, the Marquis de Sade, the utopian socialist Charles Fourier, and the author of spiritual exercises, Ignatius Loyola. In discussing ostensibly non-literary works, Barthes does not assimilate them to literature by accentuating traditional literary qualities, of style or figurative language. *Sade/Fourier/Loyola* treats these three writers as "logothetes," or creators of special "languages." Sade's exhaustive narratives of sexual adventures, Fourier's invention of a utopian society, and Loyola's prescriptions for spiritual exercises all display the same proclivity to distinguish, order, and classify; they elaborate systems which, like languages, generate signification in the domain they articulate. "There is an erotic grammar in Sade," Barthes writes, "(a pornogrammar)—with its erotemes and rules of combination,"[8] for Sadian eroticism seeks to "combine according to precise rules the specific actions of vice, so as to make from these series and groups of actions a new 'language,' no longer spoken but acted, a language of crime, or a new code of love, as elaborate as the code of courtly love" (p. 32/27).

Sade/Fourier/Loyola, like *Michelet*, and *Sur Racine*, shows the critic engaged in an activity Barthes describes in *Sur Racine*: "Let us try out on Racine, in virtue of his very silence, all the languages our century suggests"[9]. Racine is "silent" because he created forms that presume but do not determine meaning. His plays are "an empty site eternally open to signification," and if he is the greatest French author, "his genius is to be located in none of the virtues that have successively made his fortune but rather in a unrivalled art of availability, which permits him to remain eternally within the field of any critical language" (p. 11/ix). In trying out his century's languages on an author, a public experimenter is not making these works "relevant" by showing that they have something to say about current problems. That would be a thematic enterprise, emphasizing Racine's psychology of love or Michelet's political views. On the contrary, Barthes's trying out of contemporary languages generally accentuates the strangeness of the writings he treats- -Michelet's obsessions, Racine's claustrophobic universe, Sade, Fourier, and Loyola's classifying manias. None of these last three, he writes, "is bearable (*respirable*); each makes pleasure, happiness, communication, dependent upon an inflexible order or, worse still, on a system of combinations" (p. 7/3). Barthes's writing about these *oeuvres* does not discover relevant themes but seeks instead to "unglue the text" from its vision and purpose—"socialism, faith, evil"— and *steal* its language, as he puts it: "to fragment the old text of culture, knowledge, literature, and scatter its features in unrecognizable formulations, as one disguises stolen goods" (p. 15/10). An unusual program for criticism, certainly; one which would invest in strangeness rather than familiarity, and finds pleasure in fragments. Barthes is strikingly unconcerned to describe the contours or construction of individual works. In stealing the language of writers of the past, he seeks to elucidate *practices* of writing and their implications for meaning and order rather than to interpret and evaluate finished *works*.

Not only does Barthes write on marginal authors in ways that challenge the concept of literature; as a public experimenter trying out the languages his culture offers, he also works at the interstices of disciplines. Though he often delighted to propose new sciences—a science of literature, a semiology, a narratology, a science of contemporary myths, an "arthrology" or science of divisions, a typology of textual pleasures—he gave himself the writer's license to steal and exploit the language of other disciplines. *La Chambre claire*, he says, departs from "a vague, casual, even cynical phenomenology, so readily did it agree to distort or to evade its principles according to the whim of my analysis."[10] A fragmment of *Barthes par Barthes* describes this propensity in different terms:

> In relation to the systems which surround him, what is he? Say an echo chamber: he reproduces the thoughts badly, he follows the words, he pays his visits, i.e., his respects, to vocabularies, he *invokes* notions, he rehearses them under a name; he makes use of this name as of an emblem (thereby practicing a kind of philosophical ideography) and this emblem dispenses him from following to its conclusion the system of which it is the signifier (which simply makes a sign to him) [*qui simplement lui fait signe*]. Coming from psychoanalysis and seeming to remain there, "*transference*" nonetheless readily leaves the Oedpial situation. The Lacanian "*image-repertory*" [*imaginaire*] extends to the borders of the classical "self-love" [*amour-propre*] . . . "*Bourgeois*" receives the whole Marxist accent, but keeps overflowing toward the aesthetic

and the ethical. In this way, no doubt, words are shifted, systems communicate, modernity is tried (the way one tries all the push buttons on a radio one doesn't know how to work), but the intertext thereby created is literally *superficial*: one adheres *liberally*: the name (philosophic, psychoanalytic, political, scientific) retains with its original system a line which is not cut but remains: tenacious and floating. No doubt the reason for this is that one cannot at one and the same time desire a word and take it to its conclusion: in him the desire for the word prevails, but this pleasure is partly constituted by a kind of doctrinal vibration.[11]

Whatever the pleasures of liberating a term from its original system, the "doctrinal vibration" has been important to the success of Barthes's writings, and when he gives that up by inventing his own terms, abandoning the suggestive linkage to another body of discourse or another discipline, the effects are quite different. Always a lover of classifications, he used to transpose across disciplinary boundaries. In *Sur Racine*, for example, he maintained that there were three sorts of literary history: a history of literary signifieds, a history of literary signifiers, and a history of literary signification. The use of terms that belong together and are sustained by a system of thought gives the typology a logic and a plausibility, even if the terms are applied figuratively. Consider by contrast a typology from *Sollers écrivain*, where Barthes suggests that there are five ways of reading Sollers: "en piqué," "en prisé," "en déroulé," "en rase-mottes," and "en plein-ciel"—which might be crudely rendered as "in spearing," "in savoring," "in unrolling," "in nose-to-the-ground," and "in full-horizon."[12] This typology is doubly figurative: the categories are presented as if they were modes or keys (a reading "*in* full-horizon"), and they are drawn from quite different areas of discourse. They have little in common and apply in oblique ways to reading. To read "in the spearing mode" is to pick out flavorful phrases here and there; to read "in the savoring mode" is to take in fully a particular development; to read "in the unrolling mode" is to proceed swiftly and evenly, while a "nose-to-the-ground reading" progresses word-by-word, and a "full-horizon" reading takes overviews, seeing the text as an object in context. This is what one might call a disposable typology: suggestive, witty, but with no theoretical claims and little chance that others will try to integrate it in a theory of reading. It abandons the working at the boundaries that in other cases made Barthes's discourse so challenging and productive.

Finally, Barthes makes criticism a struggle against the values and boundaries that customarily delineate the literary. In *Le Plaisir du texte* he writes that "the whole effort consists of materializing the pleasure of the text, in making the text *an object of pleasure like any other* . . . . The important thing is to equalize the field of pleasure, to abolish the false opposition of practical life and contemplative life."[13] An even more striking example of an attempt to displace boundaries is his late work, *Fragments d'un discours amoureux*, which is not a thematic study of love in literature, nor an analysis of love in contemporary society, but a simulation of the discourse of love—a language spoken by millions of people, diffused in popular romances and television programs as well as in serious literature, such as Goethe's *Werther*. Writing out fragments of this language (which reflects intensely on itself) Barthes attempts to capture what is recognizable, according to the stereotypes of our culture, as a lover's complaint. And he shows special interest in what might be most devalued by literary analysis, the sentimentality of the lover's discourse. This sentimentality, "discredited by modern opinion," makes love unfashionable, even "obscene," a topic not to be discussed in polite company—unlike sex, which is accepted as an important subject of current discourse. "(Historical reversal: it is no longer the *sexual* which is indecent, it is the *sentimental*—censured in the name of what is finally only *another morality*)."[14] But the true "obscenity" of love's sentimentality lies in the fact that one cannot, by publishing sentimentality, commit a dramatic transgression, so that it remains completely beyond the pale. "The obscenity of love is extreme. Nothing can redeem it, bestow upon it the positive value of a transgression . . . The amorous text (scarcely a text at all), consists of petty narcissisms, psychological paltrinesses; it is without grandeur: or its grandeur . . . is to be unable to attain grandeur (pp. 211/178–79).

Barthes, promoter of the Marquis de Sade, had worked to create an intellectual climate attuned to transgression. To bring back the sentimentality of ordinary love, he suggests, is a transgression of transgression, a violation of the orthodoxy that values radical transgression. Writing out the figures of a neglected discourse, Barthes surprises us in *Fragments* by making love, in its most absurd and sentimental forms, an object of interest. This might be seen as a part of an ongoing project whereby Barthes's assault on the boundaries between the literary and the non-literary, and his repeated celebration of avant-garde challenges to literature, work to break the academy's hold on nineteenth-century literature so that he may eventually bring it back as a defamiliarized object of pleasure, as a source of what he calls "transgression without grandeur." By taking avant-garde literature as the model, *S/Z* and *Le Plaisir du texte*, elaborate a practice of reading which can reveal the excesses, the complications, and the subversions of what Barthes calls "la littérature française de Chateaubriand à Proust." Though he never quite got to Proust, Barthes revealed to us, for example, a new Balzac. Or again, his *Fragments d'un discours amoureux* makes the sentimental and unfashionable discourse of *Werther* an object of contemporary interest. This is no mean accomplishment, and is made possible by the interdisciplinary theoretical arguments that broke traditional criticism's hold on literature. An eloquent passage of *Leçon*, worth citing in French, explains:

> Les valeurs anciennes ne se transmettent plus, ne circulent plus, n'impressionnent plus; la littérature est désacralisée, les institutions sont impuissantes à la protéger et à l'imposer comme le modèle implicite de l'humain. Ce n'est pas, si l'on veut, que la littérature soit détruite; c'est qu'*elle n'est plus gardée*: c'est donc le moment d'y aller. La sémiologie littéraire serait ce voyage qui permet de débarquer dans un paysage libre par déshérence: ni anges ni dragons ne sont plus là pour la défendre; le regard peut alors se porter, non sans perversité, sur des choses anciennes et belles, dont le signifié est abstrait, périmé: moment à la fois décadent et prophétique, moment d'apocalypse douce, moment historique de la plus grande jouissance. (pp. 40–41)

> The old values are no longer transmitted, no longer circulate, no longer impress; literature is desacralized, institutions are impotent to defend and impose it as the implicit model of the human. It is not, if you will, that literature is destroyed; rather *it is no longer protected*: so this is the moment to go there. Literary semiology is, as it were, that journey that lands us in a country free by default; angels and dragons are no longer there to defend it. Our gaze can fall, not without perversity, upon

certain old and lovely things, whose signified is abstract, out of date. It is a moment at once decadent and prophetic, a moment of gentle apocalypse, a historical moment of the greatest possible pleasure. (pp. 474–76)

Barthes's disruption of boundaries is what provides the intelligibility of this strange moment, when what has been denigrated returns in a new guise.

Derrida has a different way of working on the boundaries but for him too they are the source of energy, in that they are the site of massive metaphysical investments: the hierarchical distinctions between mind and body, subject and object, essence and accident, nature and culture, literal and figurative, intelligible and sensible, transcendental and empirical, speech and writing, positive and negative, are boundaries by which the Western tradition has sought to establish the priority of an origin or norm seen as pure, standard, self-identical, in order then to conceive of complication, derivation, negation, accident, manifestation as supplementary. The urgency with which theorists from Plato to Saussure have set writing aside as a dangerous supplement suggests that there is much at stake in this particular boundary and that a critical discourse could gain considerable purchase from focusing on this point of intensity and investigating the structures at work in the representation of what is being set aside. Explorations of how the workings of a discourse undermine the hierarchical oppositions on which it relies do not destroy boundaries, yielding a monism in which, for example, there would be only writing, only accident, only body, only metaphor. Very schematically, the deconstruction of a hierarchical opposition involves (1) the demonstration that it is a construction or imposition by showing how an inversion of the opposition is implicit in its textual functioning, and (2) the reinscription of the inverted and displaced opposition with a different status and impact. If speech and writing are distinguished as two versions of a generalized protowriting, or "archi-writing," the opposition no longer has the same function and implication as when writing is seen as a technical and imperfect representation of speech. Or again, the distinction between the literal and the figurative works differently when the deconstructive inversion identifies literal language as figures whose figurality has been forgotten.

We can detect a difference between Derrida and Barthes here, for where Derrida is supremely sceptical about the possbility of breaking out of the discourse of metaphysics, Barthes shows a utopian strain, in his talk of breaking down boundaries: for example, his desire to make the pleasure of the text "un plaisir comme les autres." In *Barthes par Barthes* he writes of Barthes, "Obviously he dreams of a world which would be *exempt from meaning* (as one is exempt from military service). This began in *Writing Degree Zero*, which imagines 'the absence of every sign'; subsequently a thousand affirmations incidental to this dream (a propos of the avant-garde text, of Japan, of music, of the alexandrine, etc.)" (p. 90/87).

Derrida articulates no such dream and always insists on the importance of a double gesture—one must write with both hands, he maintains—a movement that critically employs the boundaries which are put in question. His writing exploit boundaries in various ways; one book is entitled *Margins of Philosophy* and opens with an introduction called *Tympan*, "Tympanum," which sets side by side a reflection on the limits of philosophy with Michel Leiris's discussion of the repercussions of the name "Persephone": a structure that sets up reverberations much as does a tympanum, a membrane that at once divides and acts as a sounding board, transmitting vibrations between the spaces it separates. *Glas* too—another book of Derrida's—exploits the boundary or space between two columns to provoke reflection on the boundaries between literature and philosophy, paternal authority and maternal relations, spirit and body, orthodoxy and heterodoxy, property and theft, as manifested principally in Hegel and Genet. Moreover, Derrida works on or at the boundaries of disciplines, demonstrating, for example, the importance of undertaking what one might call a literary reading of philosophy and philosophical reading of literature. One might say much the same of the relations of literature and linguistics or literature and psychoanalysis, for in both cases Derrida has taught us to read the theoretical discourses of a discipline as texts—as heterogeneous narrative constructions, determined by a variety of canny and uncanny exigencies. The rereading of Freud's writings as theories and examples of textuality has been one of the most productive enterprises in recent literary criticism. We have come to see how psychoanalytic narrative and psychoanalytic theory become caught up in the structures they seek to elucidate, displaying relations of transference and countertransference that prove inseparable from the quest for theoretical mastery. (One consequence of this work at the boundaries of criticism: the place to study Freud in most universities is now the English or the French department).

There are contrasts between Barthes's and Derrida's ways of working at the boundaries, but one should emphasize that if Barthes's writings evoke thematically a utopian end to boundaries and try at moments to enact that vision, they nevertheless rely quite remarkably, even perversely, on boundaries they displace. The most striking example is, of course, *S/Z*, which begins by distinguishing the readerly from the writerly (text that we know how to read because it complies with our cultural codes from text that can only be written not read and is in effect written by anyone who reads it). *S/Z* insists on the distinction and affirms that "the writerly is our value," but then proceeds to analyze a story by that most readerly of novelists, Balzac, and instead of revealing a boring predictability, opens the story up, articulating it as an astute and resourceful reflection upon its own codes. Barthes's analysis is exemplary here: structural analyses predicated upon a distinction between works that comply with conventions and works that violate them end up discovering a radical literary practice in the most unexpected places, just as analyses that begins by positing a boundary between the literary and the non-literary and setting out to describe literariness end up by articulating divisions *within* the literary and *within* the non-literary rather than a boundary between the two.

This, it seems to me, is the most general form of the contemporary lesson about boundaries: that the establishment of a boundary is an attempt to deal with a problematical internal difference by projecting it as a controllable external difference (a boundary where one could hope to live comfortably on one side or the other). The boundaries of criticism are posited in the hope that we might dwell comfortably on one side or the other, but the work of criticism involves a certain discomfort: writing about writing, say, without ever being able to get comfortably or definitively *within* what one is working on, yet without any assurance that one is in a position of mastery or exteriority, outside of and in control of the textual structures one is presuming to analyze. In *The Critical Difference* Barbara Johnson sums up the situation very nicely in a remark on the boundaries of criticism—specifically, on the boundary between criticism and literature: "The difference between literature and criticism consists perhaps only in the fact that criticism is more likely to be blind to the way in which its own critical difference from itself makes it, in the final analysis, literary."[15] That remark on boundaries, which itself illustrates something of the convolutions of boundaries, can serve as a mark of issues to which Barthian and Derridian analyses direct our critical attention.[16]

Notes

1. Barbara Herrnstein Smith, *On the Margins of Discourse* (Chicago: Univ. of Chicago Press, 1979), p. 8.

2. Smith, p. 142.

3. Jacques Derrida, "Parergon," in *La Vérité en Peinture* (Paris: Flammarion, 1978), p. 53. Eng. trans. of part II, "The Parergon," *October* 9 (1979), 3–40; hereafter cited in the text as *Parergon*. Also where two page numbers appear separated by a slash, e.g., (p 25/29), the first refers to the French original and the second to the English translation.

4. Stanley Fish, *Is There a Text in this Class?* (Cambridge, Mass.: Harvard Univ. Press, 1980), p. 346.

5. Wayne Booth, *Critical Understanding* (Chicago: Univ. of Chicago Press, 1979), p. 236.

6. *Anatomy of Criticism* (Princeton: Princeton Univ. Press, 1957), p. 5.

7. Roland Barthes, *Leçon: Leçon inaugurale de la chaire de sémiologie littéraire du Collège de France, prononcé le 7 janvier 1977* (Paris: Seuil 1978), pp. 31–32; also "Inaugural Lecture," trans. Richard Howard, in *A Barthes Reader*, ed. Susan Sontag (New York: Hill and Wang, 1982).

8. Roland Barthes, *Sade/Fourier/Loyola* (Paris: Seuil, 1971), p. 169. *Sade/Fourier/Loyola*, trans. Richard Miller (New York: Hill and Wang, 1976), p. 165.

9. Roland Barthes, *Sur Racine* (Paris: Seuil, 1963), p. 12. *On Racine,* trans. Richard Howard (New York: Hill and Wang, 1964), p. x.

10. *La Chambre claire: Note sur la photographie* (Paris: Gallimard and Seuil, 1980), p. 40. *Camera Lucida: Reflections on Photography,* trans. Richard Howard (New York: Hill and Wang, 1981), p. 20.

11. *Roland Barthes par Roland Barthes* (Paris: Seuil, 1975), p. 78. *Roland Barthes by Roland Barthes* trans. Richard Howard (New York: Hill and Wang, 1977), p. 74.

12. *Sollers écrivain* (Paris: Seuil, 1979), p. 75.

13. *Le Plaisir du texte* (Paris: Seuil, 1973). *The Pleasure of the Text,* trans. Richard Miller (New York: Hill and Wang, 1975), p. 93.

14. *Fragments d'un discours amoureux* (Paris: Seuil, 1977), p. 209. *A Lover's Discourse: Fragments* (New York: Hill and Wang, 1978), p. 177.

15. Barbara Johnson, *The Critical Difference* (Baltimore: Johns Hopkins Press, 1980), p. 12.

16. For further discussion, see my *On Deconstruction* (Ithaca: Cornell Univ. Press, 1982) and *Roland Barthes* (New York: Oxford Univ. Press, 1983).

Morton W. Bloomfield | *Response*

The richness of Professor Culler's paper makes a ten-minute response, as is called, rather silly and difficult. So I'm going to have to take certain selected portions of his talk and talk a little bit about them and then just drift off into some of my own ideas, which would be, on the whole, perhaps old-fashioned and perhaps not entirely to the taste of many of you. However, such as we have, we have. I want to begin my comments on Jonathan Culler's fascinating and helpful analysis of boundaries by stating my general position on the subject. I am perhaps not the right man to discuss a paper on such a subject because, although I agree with

Culler's opening sentence, that the concern with boundaries is indeed literary criticism, I would push it much further than that. Existence in any form must depend, to some extent, on boundaries. This belief does not imply that we must necessarily accept the traditional boundaries or that traditional boundaries are always easy to determine. But the absence of boundaries would make the world extremely difficult.

Because of their universality, boundaries or limits differ in their significance, depending on what they apply to. Boundaries are easy to determine in objects, the form of which is obvious, such as purely physical objects like houses and books. But they are most tricky when they apply to homes and writings, which you might say are inside the houses and the books and the manuscripts, where the internal symbolic dimensions are not subject to physical measurement. Internally, meaning enters in and external forces present at their creation are factors to take into consideration in trying to understand them. What the construction workers had in mind or thought about when working on the building of a house is not significant in understanding the meaning of that house, but what the architect, the owner, or the interior decorator had in mind when thinking of this house as a home is very important indeed. Also, it is they who make a house a home, rather than just a house.

Boundaries and limits are a perpetual philosophical problem, from the early creation myths through the pre-Socratic Greek philosophy and on to Plato, Aristotle, Medieval and Post-Medieval philosophy down to today with Geach and Nozick and many other modern philosophers. The topic has metaphysical, ontological, epistemological, political, social, and hermeneutic aspects. Without limits or boundaries we would not be able to understand anything. But, the interesting question is: what boundaries can homes and literature, not houses and books and manuscripts, have, if any? There must be some boundaries, of course. Otherwise we would not be able to understand them. But what boundaries are there is our question.

Let us put limits on to the subject of limits and see what we can do by focusing on Culler's approach, which is limited to the two great breakers of boundaries, Barthes and Derrida. Barthes destroys boundaries and Derrida exploits them. Yet as Culler points out towards the end of the paper, the enemies of boundaries cannot do without them. Both articulate the visions within the literary and within the non-literary, rather than observing boundaries between the two. You cannot escape having boundaries somewhere if you hope to deal with and understand things in symbolic creation. I prefer, then, boundaries that can be established with some sort of objectivity rather than by a melting down process which blurs discernable distinctions, some of which are, I must admit, fascinating.

I am not, of course, forbidding the breaking of boundaries, but I think we must distinguish between degrees of significance in boundaries. Some are more powerful than others. The distinctions between the roles of some signifiers are greater than those of others. The test comes with an answer to these questions: What is in the text and what is out of it? In some sense, everything is not in, but out. Everything not in *is* out but we can list an infinity of notions with this principle in mind. We must make some kind of limitation as to what is not in the text. I believe that the notion of the text cannot be dismissed, that it has some priority over the submerged aporias and their significances which surround it.

The problem of the ontological status of fiction has been, probably taking a long point of view, the chief theoretical question of our century, at least as far as the philosophers are concerned. It has at least been the problem which has fascinated 20th-century philosophers about literature more than any other problem. What degree of reality does art, especially literary art have? The question will probably come up again in this series, when Professor Margolis speaks here in several months' time. I remember in the late 40's, 50's and even 60's, reading articles published in philosophical journals on this question, some gathered together in a book by William Elton some twenty-five years ago. Analytic philosophers have always been interested in the ontic status of fictive characters. In fact, this speculation is the most popular kind of literary theorizing by philosophers, if we can call it such, who generally approach literature gingerly.

Boundaries are inevitable in one way or another if we believe the external world has some objectivity and I think it best to define our literary boundaries in large measure by objective criteria, by houses, rather than by homes. Because, you can have a house without a home, but you can't have a home without a house. You can have a book without a literary work but you can't have a literary work without something to preserve it, at least since literature became written rather than oral. I think that we should accept a text more or less as it appears in a manuscript or on a page. A text is not an invitation to the reader to create a literary work such as he pleases, but it does have real signifieds to which the signifiers point.

However, like the home as compared to the house, there is room for various interpretations. A text has relations with the outside world and is not something *sui generis*. It is, as Derrida stresses, made up of historical strategies and allegories and topoi, but these are not the only elements in it. It must be referential in some way. Of course, they all are fictive utterances and, for example, work as Barbara Herrnstein Smith would have it. Her example is, however, not going to solve the ontological problem which has exercised so many philosophers. The person or teller of the tale exists inside the poem or the tale. She is not a boundary. She is closer to the boundary than what she tells us about, but she is not herself the boundary. Professor Culler in his discussion of Derrida makes the point very clearly when he distinguishes a frame and a picture from an artist's boundary. Yet, at the same time, in the mechanical sense, a frame is a boundary but not a very significant one.

A text is also a general work which allows for many variants and interpretive possibilities. It reflects to some degree the uncertainties, even the contradictions of the author, but has left his hand with some approval from him. Derrida points to the contradictions in Saussure and Lèvi-Strauss and may well be right, but if you took Saussure aside and asked if he really deep down believed that the written word is independent of the oral, he would deny it. He may well be objectively wrong, but this is what he favors in spite of possible contradictions to be found in his text. Yet I would sooner assume that a written text, in spite of its genesis and in spite of the possible contradictions it embodies, has a more basic amount of approval from the author than a listing of its possible submerged contradictions which may be discovered or claim to be discovered in it. If the text is only the creation of the reader, as some would have it, then we are lost in the new Saragossa Sea. This may make some of us happy, but not, I think, most of us. Furthermore, in non-psychological ages, before Rousseau, before Werther, before Donne and Marvell, the ambiguities of texts are hard to uncover. The melting of boundaries is not helpful to the study of Shakespeare and Chaucer. A world which has few fixed boundaries is complex. The boundaries may be leapt over, but never destroyed. We can have our Barthes and Derrida and their valuable aperçus, but we must still return to a text which does have some boundaries and does cover essentially a defined ground. A text could still give up new and exciting aspects when approached differently. Culler has today made us aware of some of these. But a text of some sort we must have, even to uncover its boundaries. Loyola, Fourier, and de Sade all leap at them and I think they were right.

Joseph Margolis

What Is a Literary Text?

It's hard to say what a text is. It's particularly hard now, though it was not always so. It is even difficult to fix a text as a stable referent, so that we might be clear about its boundaries at least and then go on to formulate its nature more and more precisely.

There may be a certain charm in this sort of candor, in the apparent admission that a normally straightforward question has become unaccountably strange; that an expectable, entirely perfunctory expertise is overwhelmed, forced to acknowledge an uncertainty more troublesome than that pleasantly addressed to the usual patience and good manners of an audience that waits to see how a speaker will introduce his topic. But quite frankly the charm is also a seduction, for it hides—at the same time it affords a peep at—a deeper, untroubled assurance that the question must be approached correctly as well as of a condescension that wonders whether those invited to consider the matter are entirely prepared for it. *There* is the better candor, presumptuous though it cannot fail to be, because the question is, now, truly a strange one. First of all, it is a question on everyone's mind, perpetually nagging whoever bothers to read the theories of literature and language of our own day. Secondly, we know that any would-be answer must retreat to the more obscure. And thirdly, most symptomatically, because we move at once and without any felt awkwardness to address instead the question, What kind of question was the original question? These are the classic signs of approaching what, in the jargon, is sometimes called the problematic—of an age, or a discipline, or a particular confrontational moment in the perceived history of the human effort to understand a sector of its own intimate world.

Perhaps it would be best to lay out very plainly the serious kind of slippage that our question now invites. We could recoil decently then and approach it once again with newly acquired aplomb. Well, to risk it, we could say: It's very hard now to talk of texts and reference to texts, much easier to talk of *textuality* and *referentiality*.

Who would ever have thought so?

But what does it mean? What could it possibly mean—apart from confirming that we have moved in a double way from the obscure to the obscurer? It may not seem so, but the truth is that the retreat is meant as an advance, that turning from particular texts to apparently abstract universals is not Platonizing but its subversion, and that we are supposed to be assisted by that maneuver to tolerate the initial confusion of insistent, incompatible doctrines long enough to see our way clear to a fresh, even radically purged, new beginning. So the first task, now that we may imagine ourselves suitably protected, is to come to know the current confusion about texts and to begin to get our bearings on what seems most salient there. And the promised benefit is that our thinking about certain literary and cultural matters will have become considerably liberated and enlarged.

Now, in a certain sense, conceptual strategy is our topic. We may begin, sensibly enough, with a prudent scheme of all the possibilities regarding texts. At one pole, let us suppose, texts are taken to be well-demarcated entities with stable, discriminable properties. They need not be viewed as mere physical objects, but their identification and description are, in principle, straightforward and modelled on those of physical objects—themselves taken as paradigms. So construed, quarrels about texts are essentially confined to their internal complexity and certain ulterior uses to which they may be put; and theorists drawn in either or both directions often speak of offering *interpretations* of such texts. At the other pole, then, it is simply and flatly denied that there *are* any texts, that texts are stable, relatively unchanging, boundaried objects whose identity and nature are open only to the kind of dispute that already presupposes that disagreements may be genteelly resolved by examining the actual objects in question. The negative view holds that texts are not that kind of thing at all. Theorists of the first sort would say that they normally *refer* to particular *texts*: they claim to be able to settle the truth and falsity of given interpretations by consulting the texts themselves; and the results of their studies are supposed to enjoy a certain objectivity more or less in accord with (though perhaps logically weaker than) the sort of finding the physical sciences are thought to yield.

If we put matters thus, we are led to believe that the opposed views are simply linearly connected—as merely affirming and denying the same thesis. There *are* such oppositions in the literature and they are by no means negligible. But, currently, the strongest versions of the apparent denial contend that the very search for such features among texts is profoundly misguided and that what—now, with increasing equivocation—we still call interpretation plays a very complicated constitutive and peculiarly ephemeral role that we habitually and most misleadingly construe as referentially focused on texts in the old sense. It is in this sense, hardly explicit enough here, that one hears it sagely said nowadays that it is easier to talk of textuality and referentiality than of texts and reference. Whatever else may be meant by that dark saying, certainly we cannot deny that the intended complaint warns us of our not having quite captured—schematically—*all* the conceptual possibilities regarding the theory of texts and perhaps that there is no prospect of ever doing so. The reason, of course, is that the new objection is what is often called a second-order objection: not another dispute about a neighborly claim within a certain disciplined and shared inquiry familiarly marked by the original question ("What is a text?" "What is a nabob?" "What is hepatic decompensation?") but a higher-order question about the cognitive and methodological hows and whys and whats of certain inquiries that we have too long taken for granted. The new attack is vertical, then, and by its example means utterly to subvert the prospect of gathering together all the alternative theories that, in good time, we might consider and discard one by one on our way to an ideally satisfactory theory of texts. Such progress is meant to be denied by calling text and reference into question, that is, by calling into question the unmentioned assumptions that first led us to believe that, in *talking-about-texts*, we were actually referring—could actually refer—to texts in the spirit favored by our first model.

This much at least sets the stage. Now, consider some specimen views. The following, offered by Monroe Beardsley in a discussion candidly titled "The Authority of the Text," may well be the most sanguine statement that we can expect representing the first polar view about texts:

> The first thing required to make criticism possible is an object to be criticized—something for the critic to interpret and to judge, with its own properties against which interpretations and judgments can be checked. The Principle of Independence, as it might be called, is that literary works exist as individuals and can be distinguished from other things. . . . There is another postulate that is logically complementary to the first: that literary works are self-sufficient entities, whose properties are decisive in checking interpretations and judgments. This is sometimes called the Principle of Autonomy.[1]

Beardsley's view is in part intended in opposition to E. D. Hirsch's, that is, to the view (the so-called romantic hermeneutic view) that "a text means what its author meant"[2]—which Beardsley holds to be "not sensible" and which he dubs the "Identity Thesis." Beardsley's objections to Hirsch's view depend largely on resisting the appeal to authors' intentions—in line with Wimsatt and Beardsley's earlier, well-known, most controversial paper, "The Intentional Fallacy."[3] But the irony is that Hirsch, like Beardsley himself, maintains that a *text* is a reliable *referent* of some sort, only that it is not a "self-sufficient entity" in the sense in which Beardsley obviously means to invoke a favorable comparison with physical and perceptual objects—that *could* (we usually suppose) support a strong sense of objective truth.

Hirsch, then, actually invokes the same notion of truth and objectivity, but he does so in the spirit of a quite different tradition regarding the relation between the physical and the human sciences. *He* believes that interpretations can be objective readings of texts because, although they are not autonomous objects in Beardsley's sense, *texts are reliable referents nevertheless*. They have, on Hirsch's view, a complex intentional structure that, though not entirely explicit psychologically, is still *personal*—precisely in having internalized in a creative moment the formative powers of an enveloping historical culture. So the objectivity with which the meaning of a literary text can be fixed—or interpreted—is, for Hirsch, a bona fide function of our cognitive abilities (of, we may as well say, genuine science) determining, apparently, what an author originally meant in creating the poem or story that he has. Thus, in what amounts to a pretty counterpoint to Beardsley's thesis, Hirsch says:

> Textual meaning is not a naked given like a physical object. The text is first of all a conventional representation like a musical score, and what the score represents may be construed correctly or incorrectly. The literary text . . . does not have a special ontological status which somehow absolves the reader from the demands universally imposed by all linguistic texts of every description . . . . The text of a poem, for example, has to be constructed by the critic before it becomes a poem for him. Then it is, no doubt, an artifact with special characteristics. But before the critic construes the poem it is no artifact for him at all, and if he construes it wrongly, he will subsequently be talking about the wrong artifact, not the one represented by the text. If criticism is to be objective in any significant sense, it must be founded on a self-critical construction of textual meaning, which is to say, on objective interpretation.[4]

Now, Beardsley dismisses authors' intentions because he is persuaded that the canons of the human sciences are essentially the same as those that hold for the paradigmatic physical sciences—in spite of the fact that, in the former, we examine language and other cultural artifacts. In a word, Beardsley has subsumed the professional discipline of so-called New Criticism (at least approximately) within the methodological program of what is now called the unity of science—which was itself closely linked with the convictions of the Vienna Circle.[5] This is why *he* has no trouble answering the question, What is a text? And Hirsch, believing (contrary to Beardsley) that the canons of objective interpretation belong to an utterly different (complementary) science from that of physics, favors the so-called hermeneutic tradition moving (with significant demurrers on Hirsch's part) from Schleiermacher to Dilthey.[6] The upshot is that Beardsley and Hirsch disagree about the nature of literary texts, hence, also, about the methodology by which *their* meanings (that is, texts')—and *our* interpretations—can be objectively fixed or assessed. But neither one doubts that texts are determinate and individual, referentially reliable, possessing (in Beardsley's sense) or assignable (in Hirsch's) objectively confirmable meanings. Jointly, therefore, they represent the classic confidence of the principal traditions of the philosophy of science prior to certain subversive tendencies that have matured within the last twenty or twenty-five years.

The trouble is that, in the work of both, there already appears a certain telltale nervousness that strongly suggests their own considerable misgivings about the conceptual security of their respective theories. Beardsley, for instance, concedes both that, although he wishes to preclude appeal to authors' intentions as being essentially irrelevant to what may be found "in" a text, no one "has been foolish enough to think that the line dividing inside and outside [of a literary work of text] is 'as neat and definite as the page on which it is printed'"; that sometimes "whatever comes from without, but yet can be taken as an interesting extension of what is surely in [where no one can decisively establish what is 'in' or 'out'] may [nevertheless] be admissible [as 'in']. It merely makes a larger whole"; and, also, that "the meaning of a text can change [meanings can be acquired] after its author has died," in spite of the fact that "the literary text, in the final analysis, is the determiner of its meaning."[7] Correspondingly, Hirsch worries the problem of the hermeneutic circle, that is, the problem that the meaning of the parts of a text depend on the meaning of the whole text and that the meaning of the whole depends on the meaning of the parts. Here, he observes with perfect candor *both* that the parts must enjoy a certain "autonomy" and the genres (in terms of which whole texts are whole texts of determinate kinds) must have an essential and genuinely discoverable nature *if* textual interpretation is to be objective, *and* that these requirements cannot actually be satisfied. So, although he insists that "All understanding of verbal meaning is necessarily genre-bound" and that "A genre conception is constitutive of speaking as well as of interpreting," he also concedes (against, he says, Aristotle and the neo-Aristotelians) "the entirely metaphorical character of an entelechy when that concept is applied to a form of speech. A verbal genre has no entelechy or will of its own . . . the purpose of a genre is the communicable purpose of a particular speaker, nothing more nor less."[8] Still, "an intrinsic genre [which is] a shared type that constitutes and determines meanings" is apparently also "a mental object or . . . an idea," certainly not "a species concept that somehow defines and equates the members it subsumes"; and, although in determining an operative genre we are to concern ourselves only with "the author's subjective stance," the fact is that we must suppose that an author "submits to the convention that his willed implications must go far beyond what he explicitly knows" *and* that what we offer as a probable interpretation in accord with a projected genre is largely based on the grounds of the apparent coherence of the text that results.[9] In admitting this, Hirsch seems to believe that he is countering Hans-Georg Gadamer's thesis to the effect that *all* texts show this authorial limitation—hence, that genres (and textual meanings) cannot be saved except by substituting *historical tradition* for *authorial intent*.[10]

Suddenly, the picture has become very complicated. And yet there is a charming procession of views that we could provide that would help to collect a rather astonishing variety of contemporary theories and would launch us, at the same time, in the direction of the second polar extreme, that has so far remained unexamined. There are no interesting views that hold that literary texts are simply physical objects—perhaps for the elementary reason that no one (*pace* Hobbes, Skinner, Quine, D. M. Armstrong, Donald Davidson and their tribe) has been the least able to reduce human language to biological, neurophysiological, behavioral, or purely functional processes.[11] Language, the *sine qua non* of human culture and its most ubiquitous manifestation, remains—puzzlingly but compellingly—*sui generis*. Beardsley does not deny this, any more than Hirsch or Gadamer. But Beardsley believes he can treat texts as objects because, apparently, language may be construed as a congeries of conventional inscriptions and speech acts empirically open in a perfectly straightfoward way to forms of discernment entirely congruent with the perceptual discoveries and explanations of the physical sciences—in a way that does not reflect in any methodologically distinctive regard the cultural contingencies of interpreting agents or of what they interpret. Hirsch offers a more powerful orientation because he shows convincingly that there is an ineliminably interpretive (or hermeneutic) dimension in pretending merely to *perceive* literary texts, that there must be *some consensual, participant basis*, some sharing of an interpretive tradition within the diachronic flux of historical cultures, in virtue of which, first, even textual referents can be identified as such and, second, meanings can be reliably ascribed to them. No sooner does Hirsch make this gain, however, than his own scrupulous admission of the profoundly circular (though not vicious) feature of the hermeneutic or interpretive recovery of the meanings of texts undermines completely the secure individuation of texts themselves, the reliable accessibility of authorial intent, the realist standing of constitutive genres, and, therefore, the reassuring conceptual bulwark intended against all forms of relativism.[12] In fact, all three theorists—Beardsley, Hirsch, and Gadamer—explicitly oppose relativism.

It would be wrong to suppose, however, that subscribing to the referential determinancy of texts (or of other objects or referents) precluded every robust form of epistemic relativism; but it is certainly clear that, in the different ways they do, these authors link textual determinancy with their own objections to relativism. In fact, in shifting from the authority of authors to an informed responsiveness to historical traditions, Gadamer means to escape the threatening relativism engendered by Heidegger's emphasis on the historical contingencies of interpreting agents; for now, those agents must themselves attempt to recover (while in historical motion, so to say) the meanings of texts that also suffer the contingencies of their own historical careers. This is why Gadamer favors:

> a notion of science that does not allow for the ideal of the nonparticipating observer but endeavors instead to bring to our reflective aware-

ness the communality that binds everyone together . . . the way the being of the interpreter pertains intrinsically to the being of what is to be interpreted. Whoever wants to understand something already brings along something that anticipatorily joins him with what he wants to understand—a sustaining agreement . . . . Any understanding of another's meaning, or that of a text, is encompassed by a context of mutual agreement in and through all dissent.[13]

Here, then, at one stroke, determinate textual meanings and determinate textual referents are threatened together. Beardsley fudges the hermeneutic complexity of understanding texts when he outlaws authorial intentions. Hirsch fudges the fixity of authorial intent when he denies that genres have an essential reality. And Gadamer fudges the very possibility of textual reference and interpretive validity when he maintains that the texts we strive to understand are in a sense diachronically and unendingly constituted by every historically placed interpretive effort to speak (as Gadamer would say) to another age and to have that other age speak to us.

Now, perhaps, it begins to be clear why, at the end of this series of reflections, it is easier to speak of textuality and referentiality than of texts and reference. Gadamer opposes every attempt at methodological rigor (though he cannot but presuppose such rigor) because he believes that a true respect for the historicity of texts and for their interpretive openness to historically distant communities entails that the condition for the authentic responsiveness of such communities *to* their meanings already *includes* a fusing of the meanings of one's own historical experience with that of the other:

> When we listen to someone or read a book [it is not that] we must forget all our foremeanings concerning the content, and all our own ideas [our prejudices in effect]. All that is asked is that we remain open to the meaning of the other person or of the text. But this openness always includes our placing the other meaning in a relation with the whole of our own meanings or ourselves in a relation to it.[14]

A text, therefore, *has* no determinate meaning, in spite of the fact that there *is* a condition—an ontological condition (the fusing of historical horizons: *Horizontverschmelzung*)—that is required, though no criteria for its satisfaction can be methodologically specified, on which alone a genuine understanding of a text is made possible. A text is not a notation for safely recovering some temporally frozen meaning or truth; a text is a "construct" that emerges "eminently" in the genuine process of interpretation, but is not and cannot be exhausted or fixed by that process. It achieves "presence" by the fusion that is genuine reading, though we ourselves are forever "bound to the laws of temporality."[15]

The irony is that, in opposing Dilthey's sanguine claims about a distinctive methodology of the human sciences (including the interpretation of texts) because, on his view, such a methodology must alienate would-be interpreters from the genuine dialogue of historical horizons, Gadamer still opposes relativism—a commitment that cannot but entail a high confidence about correct criteria or about discerning a genuine fusing of *our* horizon with that of *another*. Otherwise, we could only claim to know the purely abstract condition on which we genuinely understand a text, but we could never reliably show that a particular interpretation was correct or not—even within the putative fusion of horizons. In short, in Gadamer's view, to put things crudely, there is no distinction between a text and its interpretation, every text is potentially infinite because interpretation is historicized, *and* the meaning of a text constitutively includes all of "its" authentic interpretations. Reference and validity, therefore, become methodologically insoluble puzzles; although in spite of that, Gadamer clings to what must presuppose more than his minimal ontological condition—some further condition that he actually repudiates.

We can perhaps afford a few additional specimens—deliberately drawn from quite different conceptual traditions—in order to suggest something of the power of this way of collecting views attracted to the positive pole of the theory of texts. The clue to enlarging our list of doctrines depends on the notion that, whatever we may make of it, a text cannot be completely, more or less unchangeably, "there," intact, for characterization as well as for reference: *some* weakness with respect to one or the other or both must be conceded.

To mention one specimen view: Roman Ingarden has developed a notably influential theory of texts, formulated in phenomenological terms, that pointedly addresses both issues. At one time, Ingarden held an unusually straightforward Platonist doctrine, affirming that, although (relative to a set of sentences) it did indeed "come into being," "as a purely intentional object, the literary work of art [did] not partake in the events of the real world and [was not and need never have been] drawn into their flow."[16] It's true that Ingarden gave up this extreme idealism—which threatened reference in any case. But he never gave up the notion of the fixed intentional structure of a literary work. So he held that it remained "a purely intentional object which [had] its basis of being in the creative acts of consciousness of its author"; and, although he avoided the romantic hermeneutic strategy, it was only because of his remarkably sanguine confidence in the reader's ability to recover a literary text (or better, a literary work)—unaltered and entire—from the inscribed signs of some language:

> As soon as it is fixed in an existing intersubjective language in any kind of physical material (printing, writing, tape-recording, etc.), it is in theory cognitively accessible, as a pregiven object, to any reader who has a command of reading . . . . Thus the whole work in all its strata is basically reconstructed as if anew by the reader from his own resources.[17]

Ingarden made allowance, here, for at least two sorts of tolerance. First, where inscriptions and meanings proved variable, he claimed that we favored the "typical" (which apparently yielded a sort of empirical invariance); second, where they were read and appreciated by particular readers, literary words, he said, were "concretized," that is, given unified and intentional (though variable) particularity with respect to (all) the schematic "strata" of the literary work itself (which cleverly linked the invariance of literary objects with the variability of how they were read and interpreted). But Ingarden never addressed Gadamer's problem—in effect, the problem of post-Nietzschean, post-Heideggerian historicism—of how to insure fixity of meaning and significance within the flux of human language and human culture. So his confidence about the reliability of reference, about how to decode unchanging intentions from mere physical marks, strikes us as oddly naive and vulnerable. On the other hand, his gymnastic maneuver to save the sense in which texts and their interpretations are linked to timeless literary works led to the preposterous thesis that there *were* objects that were inherently schematic, that exhibited inherent indeterminacies (*Unbestimmtheitsstellen*) that could not be removed and that were not restricted to intentional functions (as with graphs and scores), but that *could* become qualitatively and variably "concrete" (or determinate) through and only through aesthetic attention, that is, through appreciative interpretation.[18] Ingarden had to insure reference in order to insure the invariant intentional nature of literary works; but in order to accommodate the complexity of interpretive experience, he had to construe literary works as conceptual monsters.

What the mad possibilities of this line of thought are, hobbled as it is by the phenomenological insistence on the presence (or changelessness) of being can be glimpsed in the marvellously garbled view offered by René Wellek (who introduced Ingarden to American audiences) and Austin Warren:

> The work of art appears as an object of knowledge *sui generis* which has a special ontological status. It is neither real (like a statue) nor mental (like the experience of light or pain) nor ideal (like a triangle). It is a system of norms of ideal concepts which are intersubjective. They must be assumed to exist in collective ideology, changing with it, accessible only through individual mental experiences, based on the sound-structure of its sentences.[19]

This of course is an attempt to formulate Ingarden's theory manageably. Wellek and Warren needed to construe literary works as reliable referents in order to assure us that interpretations could be "verified," that "right and wrong readings" could actually be assessed as such.[20] But their own characterization utterly baffles every effort to indicate the proper procedures of interpretation; cannot facilitate qualifying and disqualifying particular interpretations (since the relevant "norms" are unpredictably changeable, never completely graspable by individual readers); and is probably incoherent in its own terms.

Wolfgang Iser affords an even more intriguing specimen, because Iser actually tries to combine the best elements of phenomenological and hermeneutic literary theory. In particular, Iser tries to combine Ingarden, Gadamer, and to a certain extent Merleau-Ponty. He adopts and adjusts Ingarden's notion of indeterminacies or gaps inhering in the literary work, which then invite the reader to "fill in" interpretively what is objectively lacking; but in place of conventional criteria for checking whether the reader's contribution is likely to be correct or accurate, Iser reverts to something like Gadamer's notion of the fusing of horizons (or to Merleau-Ponty's analogue in his structuralized phenomenology[21]). But the result is disastrous. For, at one point, holding to a strong view of the text as a determinate referent, Iser construes the Ingarden-like side of his theory as requiring *supplements* to a stable, given text; but at another, since there is no direct way to check the validity of such interpretations by appeal to the text itself, the Gadamer-like side of his theory requires that interpretation be *constitutively* incorporated *within* the text itself. Unfortunately, there can be no consistent resolution of these two views. Iser says quite plainly that "the reader's activity must be controlled in some way by the text. [But] the control cannot be as specified as in a *face-to-face situation*, equally it cannot be as determinate as a social code, which regulates social interaction." The "blanks" are in the text, and so give rise "to the reader's projections." Still, since, as Iser claims, "*the text itself cannot change* [italics added], it follows that a successful relationship between text and reader can only come about through changes in the reader's projections."[22]

The combination of these two doctrines defines Iser's version of the so-called reader-response theory of texts. Texts cannot enter into "dyadic interaction" because they cannot themselves respond like persons (though Gadamer and Heidegger almost appeal to a metaphor of the power of texts to respond). Iser also discards structuralism and the naive semiotics of Ingarden, for, rather along lines favored by Merleau-Ponty, any would-be communicative code must include what is creatively projected by the interpreting reader himself. The results leads to what is either an explicit contradiction or a doctrine impossible to distinguish in practice from that contradiction. "The text itself cannot change," Iser claims; also, the text has inherent gaps, "inherent blanks" which provoke the reader's interpretive activity or "projections." Or better, there is "an indeterminate, constitutive blank which underlies all processes of [dyadic] interactions [between text and reader]"; but "this blank is not a given, ontological fact, [it] is [instead] formed and modified by the imbalance inherent in dyadic interactions, as well as in that between text and reader." Furthermore, "the text provokes continually changing views in the reader," simply because the the perceived gaps in the text are themselves "continually reformulated as the [*reader's*] projections themselves are readjusted by their successors."[23] Once this is granted, Iser *can* no longer claim that "the reader's activity must be controlled . . . by the text," for the text must change as a result of the reader's response. On his own view:

> The text is a whole system of such processes [of reader projection], and so, clearly, there must be a place *within* this system [italics added] for the person who is to perform the reconstituting. This place is marked by the gaps in the text—it consists in the blanks which the reader is to fill in.[24]

But the gaps themselves are a function of the reader's own responses to previous responses to the would-be text; *and* the text is constituted in some sense by the reader's own projections. What we have here, at best, is a reader-response analogue of Gadamer's fusion of horizons—at worst, a flat contradiction.

One final specimen should be enough. It may not unfairly be argued that Stanley Fish has for some years been developing—in a self-consciously naive, self-critical, somewhat ironic manner— an American version of reader-response theory. Fish actually began his effort in reaction to the New Critics' acceptance of the authority of the text. (In a way, he is his own self-appointed critic. His latest book, *Is There a Text in This Class?* explicitly collects the errors of earlier papers, as Fish moves on to seemingly more tenable positions.) In any case, as he himself says: "In 1970 I was asking the question 'Is the reader or the text the source of meaning?' and the entities presupposed by the question *were* the text and the reader whose independence and stability were thus assumed."[25] The question was intended to challenge Wimsatt and Beardsley's well-known Intentional and Affective Fallacies, and to show "that the text was *not* the self-sufficient repository of meaning and . . . that something else was, at the very least, contributory." In fact, on this view, "the reader's response is not *to* the meaning: it *is* the meaning, or at least the medium in which what I wanted to call the meaning comes into being."[26] What, however, Fish discovered (what others had already found out for themselves) was that, if he really meant to argue for "a common reading experience" on the part of competent readers, then he could not distinguish in principle between his own thesis and that of the New Critical "formalists"; for the standard of *his* reader could not but be such that "his every operation [had] to be strictly controlled by the features of the text."[27] And so, as Fish himself saw, the distinction collapsed.

Like most of the theorists already examined, moreover, Fish opposed relativism, construed reading and interpretation as disciplines exhibiting a science-like rigor, and sought a formulation in accord with which the reliability of textual reference and the creative activity of interpretive readers could be reconciled. His most recent proposal for satisfying these constraints is, predictably, consistent with them but hardly strong enough to insure his principal objective. For, now, he finds himself obliged to say "that an interpreting entity, endowed with purposes and concerns, is, by virtue of its very operation, determining what counts as the facts to be observed": it turns out, ironically, "that linguistic and textual facts, rather than being the objects of interpretation, are its products."[28] Since Fish does not wish to reject "the distinction between description and interpretation"—hence, the advantage, however weakened, of textual reference—he cannot possibly hold a theory that is very much unlike Gadamer's, Ingarden's or Iser's in at least that respect in which the reader's interpretation of something provisionally called the text becomes constitutive of what eminently emerges as the text. The equivocation is essential to all our specimen views—less so for Beardsley and Hirsch, given their extremely strong commitment to determinate textual reference *and* determinate textual boundary; but even in their efforts one can detect incipient concessions in this same direction (in Hirsch: with regard to his fiddling between "interpretation" and "significance"[29]; in Beardsley: with regard to the special complications associated with what he calls the "presentation of an aesthetic object"[30]).

In Fish, the latest innovation is to undercut the independence of both text *and* reader. The formula—which Fish himself recognizes threatens to favor both subjectivism and relativism—construes literary texts as the conventional posits of a functioning community and individual readers as those who share a certain collective process of deciding matters of importance:

> The act of recognizing literature is not constrained by something in the text, nor does it issue from an independent and arbitrary will: rather, it proceeds from a collective decision as to what will count as literature, a decision that will be in force only so long as a community of readers or believers continues to abide by it.[31]

Hence, as Fish quite candidly affirms: "There is no single way of reading that is correct or natural, only 'ways of reading' that are extensions of community perspectives . . . the entities that were once seen as competing for the right to constrain interpretation (text, reader, author) are now all seen to be the products of interpretation."[32]

"I preserved generality by rhetoricizing it," Fish says.[33] Yes, of course, but in the process Fish neglected to say what the operative boundaries of functioning communities are, what might *legitimate* the interpretive practices of any small group *as a bona fide community* (Fish, persuasive in his own classroom, for instance). Without such an account, there is no way to disqualify collective blindness, collective distortion, false consciousness, superstition, or sheer illiteracy. Relativism and subjectivism of the worst sort could not then be discounted. On the other hand, *if* there are legitimate constraints on interpretation, then Fish requires a richer theory than he supplies—perhaps along Gadamer's, or Marx's, or Wittgenstein's lines. Fish himself had been attracted at one time to the sort of universal linguistic constraints that Chomsky has favored; but he now finds such accounts seriously defective, and he is frank to suggest that whoever would rally to his own readings of literary texts would probably count as as good an interpretive community as any other.[34]

So far, we have permitted ourselves to be drawn along, in a reasonably natural but relaxed way, among certain salient, more or less companionable specimens attracted to what we have called the positive pole of literary theory. They form a sort of continuum from, say, Beardsley's thesis to Fish's latest pronouncement: their principle of individuation, one might claim, lies with the measure of their commitment jointly to the referential independence of texts (as objects of interpretation) and to the explicitness of the boundaries of texts themselves (as constraints on the validity of interpretation). Comparison, here, is straightforwardly linear. What we must now consider are certain more drastic intrusions into the rather idyllic atmosphere of the succession of theories we've sampled—vertical disruptions, so to say, that reject any foundation on which a progressively more adequate theory may be hoped for. In fact, even without the minuet of theories already examined, we cannot fail to have noticed a certain constant threat of incoherence, of retreat from the issues, or mere rhetoric, of desperate measures.

The change in direction is more disjunctive, however. The increasing diffuseness of Gadamer, Ingarden, Wellek, Iser, and Fish represents an increased wariness about the complexity of the task of defining a literary text: the notions of reference and textual boundary begin to slip away—with noticeable reluctance and weariness on the part of their sponsors. But though the champions of the negative pole (as we might call them) appear merely to continue the fatal dissection of the entire enterprise, albeit with considerable relish, the truth is that they mean to abandon in a most radical way the assumptions, definitions, presuppositions, presumptions—in a word, the philosophical faith—of the partisans of the opposite pole. It is an irony that this subversive orientation should, in a sense, be traceable to the convergent influence of a number of powerful thinkers who were themselves very strongly committed to the prospects of various sorts of human science—an influence probably most economically focused in the work of Ferdinand de Saussure and Edmund Husserl; and yet each of these thinkers betrayed such an essential uneasiness about the viability and coherence of their own respective ventures that one could easily believe, in retrospect, that the radical reproof of their undertakings could be fairly traced to their own convictions: against Saussure, that the so-called structuralist system he called *langue* could never, on his own view, map the living utterance of language, which he called *parole*; against Husserl, that the so-called phenomenological reduction of human knowledge could never be separated, as he always pretended was possible (and necessary), from the sheer contingencies of subjective or empirical psychology. The radical implications of recovering this discovery are most clearly drawn from the self-criticism of Roland Barthes and the much more ambitious and more florid deconstructions of Jacques Derrida.

But the path is somewhat indirect. At the risk of obvious distortion, structuralism first applied to natural language, then for all communicative systems (for instance, by Lévi-Strauss), may be encapsulated in the following remark of Saussure's:

> . . . in language there are only differences. Even more important: a difference generally implies positive terms between which the difference is set up; but in language there are only differences *without positive terms*. Whether we take the signified or the signifier, language has neither ideas nor sounds that existed before the linguistic system, but only conceptual and phonic differences that have issued from the system . . . . A linguistic system is a series of differences of sound combined with a series of differences of ideas.[35]

Roughly, in Saussure's hands, the actual utterances of natural language (*parole*) are unsystematizable (in effect, unintelligible) and so must be replaced (for the sake of science) by an idealized network of signs (*langue*) fitted as well as possible and always in need of diachronic adjustment. What results is a *system* in the multiple sense: first, that the would-be elements are only *relata* and function as they do only in relation to the same system; second, that the resulting network is synchronic, timeless, merely conceptual; third, that the network is designed to totalize, that is, to provide rules for generating all possible forms of intelligible structure within the domain analyzed; and finally, that language in this sense belongs only to a society as a whole and cannot have been internalized by any apt speaker. Against this background, Roland Barthes appears as that remarkably agile theorist who serially manages (compellingly and progressively against his earlier selves), first, to advocate the study of the rules of the system of narrative texts to the exclusion of particular texts; second, to treat every text as generated by and only by its own system; and third, to break through all such pretensions that keep us from the real world, to the infinite intertextuality of all texts and utterances.³⁶

We may glimpse the radical quality of Barthes' mature view from his dialectical use of the notions of "work" and "text":

> The theory of the text is directly critical of any metalanguage: revising the discourse of scientificity, it demands a mutation in science itself, since the human sciences have hitherto never called into question their own languge, which they have considered as a mere instrument or as purely transparent.³⁷

> . . . the work is concrete, occupying a portion of book-space (in a library, for example); the Text, on the other hand, is a methodological field . . . . While the work is held in the hand, the text is held in language: it exists only as discourse. The Text is not the decomposition of the work; rather it is the work that is the Text's imaginary tail . . . . The work itself functions as a general sign and thus represents an institutional category of the civilization of the Sign [the work becomes the object of a "science of the letter"]. The text, on the contrary, practices the infinite deferral of the signified: the Text is *dilatory*; its field is that of the signifier ["decentered, without closure," radically "plural"].³⁸

What Barthes means is that there *is* no text to be confronted and then interpreted: to pretend that there is is to form a work as a stable referent by focusing on some "part" of the seamless field of the textual—in order to submit it, thus boundaried, to the would-be rules of semiology. In effect, Text is the whole of writing or utterance, which may be "cut" into "works" by imposing any of an indefinite variety of principles of authorship, theme, genre, era, and the like—all external and arbitrary, however contingently useful.³⁹ This is the meaning of that otherwise impenetrably brilliant summary of Barthes' final thesis:

> Every text, being itself the intertext of another text, belongs to the intertextual, which must not be confused with a text's origins: to search for the "source of" and "influence upon" a work is to satisfy the myth of filiation.⁴⁰

There is no science of the Text; there is no type of the Text; there is no source or origin of the Text; there *is* no Text. To put the point more mildly—though not less radically—the idiom of referentially stable, individuated objects is the work of a variously practical imposition of some semiotic network that aspires to be a Saussurean system of structures; and the idiom itself is responsible for the false impression that the things of the humanly encountered world are simply transparently thus encountered as individually present to our perception.

This, precisely, is the point of Derrida's linkage of Saussure and Husserl (and even Heidegger) within the thrall of the "philosophy of presence," of "logocentrism," of "onto-theology," of the whole Western trance about the adequation of thought and being.[41] The full influence of Barthes on Derrida and Derrida on Barthes is neither clear nor crucial here. But Derrida, more than Barthes, saw the convergence of Saussure and Husserl within the common, irresistible master metaphysics of the Western tradition as signalling a bewitchment of thought that must forever be battled—though only (since there can be no other access) from *within* that language of structured being. This is the work of "deconstruction" and at least one of the important uses of that curious mark "*différance*," that Derrida says "is *neither* a word nor a *concept*."[42] Of course, if it were a word or a concept, it would fall fatally within the metaphysical network that its use is intended to undermine. The irony is that it cannot be said, or indicated, or referred to, or characterized. Its use is a parasitic, inarticulable but intentional activity that subverts our habit of relying on the structured differences of *any* conceptual scheme. It exposes foundations, origins, kinds of being, particulars, determinate existence, reference, natures, meanings as committed to some totalized and necessary system—which we can actually never recover or validate and which we chase in thought by tracing the "absent traces" of some supposed system (the Saussurean-like differences or *relata* that, in theory, are required to give any distinctions their meaning). There is no limit to such supposed systems of traces: they cannot be totalized and we cannot discover their originary source—there is none.

From this point of view, Husserl is simply the most persistent, perhaps the most uncompromisingly explicit, philosopher of being—heir of course to the entire Western tradition, and not as coy or duplicitous (however innocently) as Heidegger. There seem to be no stunningly elementary statements of Husserl's own conception of phenomenology. Roughly, then, within the same benign distortion accorded to Saussure, Heidegger could be said to hold that it is being that makes thinking possible, and Husserl could be said to hold that thinking is impossible without thinking being. Husserl is more radically devoted to the originary capacity of human thought. In this spirit, then, we may risk citing a dense passage from Husserl's famous contribution to the 1927 *Encyclopedia Britannica*:

> The universal epoche of the world as it becomes known in consciousness (the "putting it into brackets") shuts out from the phenomenological field the world as it exists for the subject in simple absoluteness; its place, however, is taken by the world as given in *consciousness* (perceived, remembered, judged, thought, valued, etc.)—the world *as such*, the "world in brackets," or in other words, the world, or rather individual things in the world as absolute, are replaced by the respective meaning of each in *consciousness* [*Bewusstseinssinn*] in its various modes (perceptual meaning, recollected meaning, and so on).[43]

Here, one can almost see the emergence of structuralism from the Husserlian undertaking—*and*, at the same time, the source of its trust in otherwise invented systems of differences. For with phenomenological bracketing, Husserl firmly believes that a certain extraordinary and unsuspected power,

> transcendental subjectivity, makes its appearance as the mediating ego, which finds itself as the absolute and ultimate presupposition for everything that is at all and that now no longer finds itself as man in the world but as the ego in whom just as the world in general this man receives his sense of being. As this ego and only as such am I apodictically certain for myself and am ultimate presupposition of being to whom everything that is meaningful for me is relative.[44]

It is this presumption that Derrida finds naively articulated in Saussure's structuralism—which, therefore, affects our conception of texts as of every "object" of discourse. Hence, in his sustained criticism of Saussure (and of Rousseau and his heir, Lévi-Strauss), Derrida says: "My quarry is not primarily Ferdinand de Saussure's intention or motivation, but rather the entire uncritical tradition which he inherits [that is, the metaphysics fixed most recently in

Husserl and Heidegger] . . . . My justification would be [that the deconstruction of Saussure's system—of the transcendental signified[45]] already give[s] us the assured means of broaching the de-construction of the *greatest* totality—the concept of the *episteme* and logocentric metaphysics—within which are produced, without ever posing the radical question of writing [that is, of how communicative systems can possibly function without an originary source—*contra* both Saussure and Husserl], all the Western methods of analysis, explication, reading, or interpretation."[46] On Derrida's view, even history is suspect, since the very notion of historical sources and influences presupposes some foundational access to the structures within which what is thus identified is thus identified.[47]

And so, at long last, Derrida joins Barthes, but now in an incomparably richer conceptual setting. A new concept of writing is emerging—perhaps it is called a "concept" only to confirm its peculiarly subversive stance, its incapacity to be fully stated in the idiom (Saussure's, Husserl's, Heidegger's) it deconstructs:

> This interweaving, this textile, is the *text* produced only in the transformation of another text. Nothing, neither among the elements or within the system, is anywhere ever simply present or absent. There are only, everwhere, differences and traces of traces.[48]

And these traces depend on the generative play of *différance*, the power that confirms that no system of differences is total, closed, grasped, grounded, originary, or timeless, and that *différance* "itself" cannot be meaningfully incorporated into any such system.

Having come this far, we must now bring things to an abrupt close. The disciples of the negative pole have bequeathed us a new *aporia*, that is, an insoluble paradox generated by their own mode of clarification. Geoffrey Hartman observes, in his attempt to assist us to understand Derrida, "that we are still endeavoring to convert thinking to the fact that texts exist."[49] But if we look quite carefully at Derrida's maneuver, we cannot fail to see that he does not actually reject reference and text; he merely warns us of the *radical* provisionality of all distinctions with respect to them. He never replaces the alleged logocentric idiom. Apparently there is no other; and yet, the warning *is* effective and depends on our ability to *use* that idiom, to be caught in its systematic snares, and to escape because we understand the sense in which we cannot but be ensnared. Barthes is ensnared. Derrida is ensnared; Hartman is ensnared. Surely, Hartman's wording makes it quite clear that we may know and believe that there *are* no texts, even as we practice *referring to texts*. So the logocentric idiom *need not* be committed to any apodictic certainties about metaphysical presence. Barthes has escaped; Derrida has escaped; Hartman has escaped; and we have escaped.

In a word, Derrida is caught in a dilemma of his own playful choosing: his message cannot be stated, since if it is it must exhibit the very disorder it would relieve us of; but if it cannot be stated, we cannot say what we have learned from it—and we *have* learned from it. Furthermore, what we have learned is essentially how to make as resilient as imaginable whatever we may theorize (since we must theorize) is, for the interval of our reflection, the most perspicuous way of construing a text. But that means that we must ultimately return to the project of the advocates of the positive pole. There is no other project: the work of those at the negative pole is merely the shadow of the work of the others. And talk about referentiality and textuality is simply a hyper-careful way of talking about reference and text.[50]

Notes

1. Monroe C. Beardsley, *The Possibility of Criticism* (Detroit: Wayne State Univ. Press, 1970), p. 16.

2. E. D. Hirsch, Jr., *The Validity of Interpretation* (New Haven: Yale Univ. Press, 1967), p. 1.

3. A discussion of the entire issue is given in Joseph Margolis, *Art and Philosophy* (Atlantic Highlands: Humanities Press, 1980).

4. Hirsch, "Appendix I: Objective Interpretation," *op. cit.*, p. 210.

5. Cf. Joseph Margolis, "Schlick and Carnap on the Problem of Psychology," in *Rationality and Science*, ed. Eugene T. Gadol (Vienna: Springer-Verlag, 1982); and "Relativism, History and the Objectivity of the Human Studies," *Journal for the Theory of Social Behavior*, forthcoming.

6. I have tried to preserve the distinction in a way sympathetic to both the genuine discoveries of the hermeneutic tradition and to the require-

ments of a coherent and unified account of human cognition, in "Relativism, History, and the Objectivity of the Human Studies."

7. *Op. cit.*, "The Authority of the Text."

8. *Op. cit.*, Ch. 3.

9. *Ibid.*, Ch. 3 and Appendix III.

10. *Ibid.*, p. 123ff. and Appendix II. Cf. Hans-Georg Gadamer, *Truth and Method*, trans. from 2nd ed. Garrett Barden and John Cumming (New York: Seabury Press, 1975).

11. For an extended discussion of the underlying issues, see Joseph Margolis, *Philosophy of Psychology* (Englewood Cliffs: Prentice-Hall, 1984).

12. On relativism, see Joseph Margolis, *Art and Philosophy*, Pt. Two: and "The Nature and Strategies of Relativism," *Mind*, forthcoming.

13. Hans-Georg Gadamer, "Hermeneutics as a Theoretical and Practical Task," *Reason in the Age of Science*, trans. Frederick G. Lawrence (Cambridge: MIT Press, 1981), pp. 135–136.

14. *Truth and Method*, p. 238. Cf. Hirsch, *op. cit.*, Appendix II; and Paul Ricoeur, *Hermeneutics and the Human Sciences*, trans. John B. Thompson (Cambridge: Cambridge Univ. Press, 1981).

15. Hans-Georg Gadamer, "The Eminent Text and Its Truth," trans. Geoffrey Waite, *The Horizon of Literature*, ed. Paul Hernadi (Lincoln: Univ. of Nebraska Press, 1982).

16. Roman Ingarden, *The Literary Work of Art*, trans. George G. Grabowicz (Evanston: Northwestern Univ. Press, 1973), p. 345.

17. Roman Ingarden, *The Cognition of the Literary Work of Art*, trans. Ruth Ann Crowley and Kenneth R. Olson (Evanston: Northwestern Univ. Press, 1973), p. 335.

18. *The Literary Work of Art*, p. 251.

19. René Wellek and Austin Warren, "The Mode of Existence of the Literary Work of Art," *Theory of Literature*, 2nd ed. (New York: Harcourt, Brace, 1956).

20. Cf. René Wellek, *Concepts of Criticism* (New Haven: Yale Univ. Press, 1965).

21. Cf. Maurice Merleau-Ponty, "Eye and Mind," trans. Carleton Dallery, *The Primacy of Perception*, ed. James M. Edie (Evanston: Northwestern Univ. Press, 1964); cited by Wolfgang Iser, *The Act of Reading* (Baltimore: Johns Hopkins Press, 1978).

22. Iser, *op cit.*, p. 167.

23. *Ibid.*

24. *Ibid.*, p. 169.

25. Stanley Fish, "Introduction, or How I Stopped Worrying and Learned to Love Interpretation," *Is There a Text in This Class?* (Cambridge: Harvard Univ. Press, 1980), p. 1.

26. *Ibid.*, pp. 2, 3; cf. Fish, "Literature in the Reader: Affective Stylistics," *loc. cit.*

27. *Ibid.*, p. 7. Iser discusses Fish briefly; cf. *op. cit.*, pp. 30–32.

28. *Ibid.*, pp. 8, 9.

29. *Op. cit.*, p. 8 and *passim*.

30. Beardsley, *Aesthetics* (New York: Harcourt, Brace, 1958), pp. 44ff.

31. *Op. cit.*, p. 11.

32. *Ibid.*, p. 16.

33. *Ibid.*

34. Cf. "What Is Stylistics and Why Are They Saying Such Terrible Things About It? Part II," *loc. cit.*

35. Ferdinand de Saussure, *Course in General Linguistics*, trans. Wade Baskin, ed. Charles Bally *et al.* (New York: McGraw-Hill, 1966), p. 120. For the sake of providing a brief clue (but only that) to further implications of the structuralist issues here considered, it is worth noting that the Czech structuralist movement was very strongly oriented in a similar way, except that it specifically opposed Saussure in contrasting *langue* and *parole* and deliberately emphasized that diachrony and evolution with respect to language (hence, with respect to literature) could not be excluded from or opposed to synchronic and structurally systematic studies of language. Cf. for instance, The Prague Linguistic Circle, "Theses Presented to the First Congress of Slavic Philologists in Prague, 1929," and Jan Mukařovský, "Structuralism in Aesthetics and in Literary Studies," in *The Prague School; Selecting Writings, 1929–1946*, ed. Peter Steiner (Austin: Univ. of Texas Press, 1982).

36. See Roland Barthes, "The Structuralist Activity," *Critical Essays*, trans. Richard Howard (Evanston: Northwestern Univ. Press, 1972); *Elements of Semiology*, trans. Annette Lavers and Colin Smith (New York: Hill and Wang, 1964); *S/Z*, trans. Richard Miller (New York: Hill and Wang, 1974); "A Conversation with Roland Barthes," in *Signs of the Times*, ed. Stephen Heath, Colin McCabe and Christopher Prendergast (Cambridge: Granta, 1971); "Theory of the Text," in *Untying the Text*, ed. Robert Young, (London: Routledge and Kegan Paul, 1981); "From

Work to Text," in *Textual Strategies*, ed. Josué V. Harari (Ithaca: Cornell Univ. Press, 1979).

37. "Theory of the Text," p. 35.

38. "From Work to Text," pp. 74–76.

39. Cf. Michel Foucault, "What is an Author?" in Harari, *Textual Strategies*; and "The Discourse on Language," trans. Rupert Sawyer, published with *The Archaeology of Knowledge*, trans. A. M. Sheridan Smith (New York: Harper and Row, 1972).

40. "From Work to Text," p. 77.

41. See Jacques Derrida, *Speech and Phenomena and Other Essays on Husserl's Theory of Signs*, trans. David R. Allison (Evanston: Northwestern Univ. Press, 1973); *Of Grammatology*, trans. Gayatri Chakravorty Spivak (Baltimore: Johns Hopkins Press, 1976).

42. Jacques Derrida, "Differance," in *Speech and Phenomena*, p. 130.

43. Edmund Husserl, "Phenomenology," rev. trans. Richard E. Palmer, in *Husserl: Shorter Works*, ed. Peter McCormick and Frederick Elliston (Brighton: Harvester Press, 1981), p. 24.

44. Edmund Husserl, "Syllabus for the Paris Lectures on 'Introduction to Transcendental Phenomenology,'" trans. Herbert Spiegelberg, in McCormick and Ellison, *op. cit.*, p. 79.

45. Cf. Jacques Derrida, "Semiology and Grammatology," in *Positions*, trans. Alan Bass (Chicago: Univ. of Chicago Press, 1981), p. 20. *Of Grammatology*, pp. 45–46. I have combined the material cited. The discussion of Rousseau and Lévi-Strauss appears in Pt. II, *Of Grammatology*.

46. Cf. Jacques Derrida, "The Supplement of Copula: Philosophy *Before* Linguistics," in Harari, *Textual Strategies*.

47. "Semiology and Grammatology," p. 26.

48. *Ibid.*, p. 27.

49. Geoffrey H. Hartman, *Saving the Text* (Baltimore: Johns Hopkins Press, 1981), p. xv.

50. I should like to draw the reader's attention to the distinct convergence between the account here offered and that of my respondent, Susan R. Suleiman, in her "Introduction: Varieties of Audience-Oriented Criticism," in *The Reader in the Text*, ed. Susan R. Suleiman and Inge Crosman (Princeton: Princeton Univ. Press, 1980). There are differences and at least implicit disagreements between us, which it would be inap-

propriate to pursue here. But I confess that I had quite forgotten her discussion, and I am sure that there's a good chance that it helped me form my own views.

Susan Rubin Suleiman | Response

I shall present my remarks in two stages: first focusing on some of the questions and arguments presented in Joseph Margolis's text, and then raising a few further questions of my own.

Let me start at the beginning: "What is a Literary Text? It's hard to say what a text is." Between the question that figures as title, and the first sentence that functions grammatically as an answer—even though, of course, it is not an answer at all, but a statement pointing to the difficulty, if not the impossiblity, of formulating an answer (I shall come back to that)—something not insignificant has dropped out: the adjective "literary." I point this out not because it is a fault, but rather because it is symptomatic, I think, of the evolution of critical theory over the past twenty years or so—and if one went back to the Russian Formalists, one could even say the past half century and more. The energizing question, for the Russian Formalists and for what I have elsewhere called the "first wave" of the French structuralists,[1] was precisely the question of what makes a text literary: what specifiable features do certain texts possess that allow us to define them as literature—in other words, what constitutes that element of a text which we call literariness?

The fruitfulness of this question can be judged by the number and the quality of the writings that it inspired—one of the best-known of these being Roman Jakobson's 1960 essay, "Linguistics and Poetics." In this essay Jakobson proposed the elegant—if somewhat circular—definition of the poetic text (understood in the broad sense of literary text) as one in which the poetic function predominates, and the even more elegant definition of the poetic function as that element of a text which foregrounds "the palpability of signs" by projecting "the principle of equivalence from the axis of selection into the axis of combination."[2] The attractiveness of this formulation is that it allows us to designate certain texts as permanently and unchangingly—or essentially—literary. Literariness is seen here as a *fixed property* of certain texts. But that is precisely the vulnerable spot of the formulation as well—for it is quite clear that over the course of history some texts have been seen now as literary, now as not. Gérard Genette noted, a few years after the Jakobson essay, that "every written text has the potential of being or not being literature, according to whether it is received (primarily) as spectacle or (primarily) as message." According to this view, literariness ("spectacle-ness") is not an inherent quality of certain texts but a *variable function* that may "invest or divest in turn any object of writing."[3] In other words, what makes a text literary is that it is *read* as literature—and what qualifies as literature varies from one time and place to another. This argument has been taken up and developed by several American theorists in recent years—notably by Stanley Fish, in the essay entitled "How to Recognize a Poem When You See One," and by Mary Louise Pratt in her critique of what she calls the "poetic language fallacy," in *Toward a Speech Act Theory of Literary Discourse*.[4]

Now I would suggest that this dissolving of literariness as a fixed characteristic, and this emphasizing of the role of the *context* and the role of the *receiver* in defining what literature is—or is not—is in a sense the analogue of Joe Margolis's dropping the word "literary" as he moved from his title to his first sentence; and this dropping is in turn symptomatic of the general movement of contemporary critical theory. In the current state of affairs, the really urgent question has become, not "What is a *literary* text?" but "What is *a* text?," or better still: "Is there (such a thing as) *a* text?, and if so, how is one to read it (or them)?"

This is the question that Margolis addresses in his essay—and I hardly need point out that it is an eminently philosophical question, which makes it all the more appropriate that a philosopher should deal with it.

How, in fact, does Margolis deal with it? Certainly not by answering it outright! "It's difficult to say what a text is." Paul Ricoeur, in an essay by a very similar title, "What Is a Text?", proposed a disarmingly simple definition which he then went on to complicate: "A text is a discourse fixed by writing."[5] Margolis begins already with the complication, and then proceeds to show just how difficult it is to say what a text is by discussing a number of "specimen views" whose impasses and self-contradictions become the very matter of his argument.

The idea of grouping these specimen views around a "more or less positive" and a "radically negative" pole is not surprising—I confess, indeed, that I found it almost too familiar a strategy. What I find provocative, however, is the strategy of putting together at the "positive" pole such unlikely bedfellows as E. D. Hirsch, Jr. and Hans-Georg Gadamer, or even more so Hirsch and Stanley Fish. Hirsch appended a detailed critique of Gadamer to his book, *Validity in Interpretation* (New Haven, 1967), in which he situated Gadamer firmly in the lineage of the so-called "new Hermeneutics" (following out of Nietzsche and Heidegger), whereas he situated himself in the "old"—or let's say "traditional"—hermeneutical tradition of Schleiermacher and Dilthey. As for Fish, it has become almost a commonplace to evoke Hirsch and Fish as the prime representatives of two irreconcilable views concerning text and interpretation. Their names have become metonyms for the "authoritarian" vs. the "relativist" positions.

Margolis actually makes a good case, I think, for including Gadamer among his "positive specimens," on the grounds that Gadamer, like Hirsch, opposes relativism. I have greater difficulty with his inclusion of Fish in this category, even if he places him at the outer reaches of it. Fish is a slippery figure, of course, as he himself is the first to proclaim; certainly his earlier work would fit into Margolis's "positive" category[6]—but I don't quite see how Fish's essays after "Interpreting the Variorum" support Margolis's contention about the "positive" specimens that they all to *some* degree have a commitment "jointly to the referential independence of texts (as objects of interpretation) and to the explicitness of the boundaries of texts themselves (as constraints on the validity of interpretation)." I do not think that Fish would subscribe to this view today. Nor does it seem to me quite convincing to include Fish among those for whom "the notions of reference and textual boundary begin to slip away—with noticeable reluctance and weariness on the part of their sponsors." Whatever one thinks of Fish, he certainly never comes across as reluctant or as weary. It can strike one as downright irritating, in fact, how un-anxious he is about the relativism of all interpretation!

This little disagreement apart, what I find particularly interesting in Margolis's presentation is the suggestion that there may not in fact *be* any unproblematical arguments for the "positive" view that "texts are . . . well-demarcated entities with stable, discriminable properties." As Margolis shows, Hirsch, Iser, Gadamer—and even Beardsley, who seems the most categorical in his defense of the authority of the text—turn out to "fudge" certain difficult issues and concede "some weakness" in their own arguments; in other words, like any text worth its salt, their texts ultimately deconstruct themselves. (Question: Does that make them literary?)

As for Margolis's "negative" exemplars, Barthes and Derrida, there is not much I want to say other than that Margolis is undoubtedly right in insisting on the radically subversive implications of their views. I think it would be interesting to look at Barthes' and Derrida's notions about the text not only in the context of European philosophy and linguistics, but also (perhaps above all) in the context of European avant-garde movements of this century. One statement I would ask Joe Margolis to develop is his final statement, that "we must ultimately return to the project of the advocates of the positive pole. There is no other project." Is this Margolis's real answer to the question of his title? If so, it is a provocative idea about which I would like to hear more.

In conclusion, I would like to raise, very quickly, a few further questions that we might ponder and that were inspired by my reading of Margolis's essay.

First, coming back to the earlier discussion of literariness, to what extent does the question of "fixed characteristics *versus* variable function" affect not only the general category of literature but also the subcategories of literary genres? Are generic traits inherent in texts, or are they metatextual categories brought to bear on certain texts that allow for a certain kind of reading? The second possibility would mean that a given text could be read in terms of more than one genre—that the notion of genre, like that of literature, is not a stable but a variable notion.

Second, and following upon the question of genre, we might ponder an idea that was treated in the present lecture series by Jonathan Culler, and that Barthes proposed in an essay quoted by Margolis, "From Work to Text"—namely, that the chief characteristic of the "plural" text (for that is what Barthes had in mind when he opposed "work" to "text," in more or less parallel fashion to his better known opposition between the "readerly" and the "writerly" text) is its situating itself "beyond the limit of doxa" or accepted opinion.[7] The really interesting texts, if we accept this view, are those that lie "outside"—those impure, hybrid, paradoxical writings that do not fit within any single generic (or, as the example of Georges Bataille, among others, suggests, any single moral or ethical) category. This is precisely where Barthes' notion of the text joins what might be called, somewhat paradoxically, the "mainstream" of avant-garde movements of this century, whose valorization of the transgressive and the marginal is perhaps their single most characteristic strategy.

Finally, and perhaps most importantly, we might—really should—raise the question of the pertinence of theoretical discussions such as ours for the related activities of teachng and evaluation. For in our role as teachers, when we ask "What is a Text?" or "What is a Literary Text?," what we are really asking, it seems to me, is "What is a text worthy of being taught, and how should one go about teaching it?" But there we have the material for a whole other colloquium.

Notes

1. See my "Introduction: Varieties of Audience-Oriented Criticism," in *The Reader in the Text: Essays on Audience and Interpretation*, ed. Susan R. Suleiman and Inge Crossman (Princeton: Princeton Univ. Press, 1980), pp. 12–13.

2. R. Jakobson, "Linguistics and Poetics," in *Style in Language*, ed. Thomas A. Sebeok (Cambridge, Mass.: MIT Press, 1960), p. 358.

3. Gérard Genette, "Structuralisme et critique littéraire," in *Figures* (Paris: Editions du Seuil, 1966), p. 146 (My translation).

4. Stanley Fish, *Is There a Text in this Class?* (Cambridge, Mass.: Harvard Univ. Press, 1980), pp. 322–338; and Mary Louise Pratt, *Toward a Speech Act Theory of Literary Discourse* (Bloomington: Indiana Univ. Press, 1977), pp. 3–37.

5. Paul Ricoeur, "Qu'est-ce qu'un texte?," in *Hermeneutik und Dïalektik II*, ed. R. Bubner, K. Cramer, R. Wiehl (Tubingen: Mohr (Siebeck), 1970), p. 181 (My translation).

6. Stanley Fish, *Surprised by Sin: The Reader in 'Paradise Lost'* (Berkeley: Univ. of California Press, 1971) and *Self-Consuming Artifacts: The Experiencé of Seventeenth-Century Literature* (Berkeley: Univ. of California Press, 1972). Fish's essay, "Interpreting the Variorum" (1976), is reprinted in *Is There a Text in this Class?*

7. "From Work to Text," in *Image, Music, Text*, trans. and ed. Stephen Heath (New York: Hill and Wang, 1977), pp. 155–164.